The Enchanted World
DRAGONS

The Enchanted World

DRAGONS

by the Editors of Time-Life Books

The Content

Time-Life Books · Alexandria, Virginia

Chapter One

Chaos Incarnate

One day long years ago, in the time when heroes ruled the Northern lands, a ragged figure could be seen scrambling along a rocky Scandinavian shore, seeking a way up the cliff that fringed the sea. He was a slave running from his master, a lord of the kingdom of the Geats. No record of his name survives, but this little man set great events in motion.

The fugitive found a path upward and climbed fast, until the wooden palisades and high-roofed chieftain's hall of the settlement he had fled seemed as small as scattered toys in the distance, and the many-oared Geatish longboats were mere specks on the shore. The shrieking of gannets and thud of the gray waves grew faint, and soon he heard only his own labored breathing and the moan of the wind. At last he reached the top, and there he paused. He was near the tip of a headland, a desolate wilderness of rock and wind-flattened grass. Directly before him stood a tumulus – the funeral mound, it seemed, of some forgotten king. The structure was immense, a pile of stone worn smooth by centuries of Northern frosts and gales. The fugitive made for it. He found the entrance, a gaping hole surrounded by a litter of black-ened rocks. Peering cautiously in, he saw a dark, downward-sloping passage. After some hesitation, the man entered the mouth of the grave – and was plunged into darkness. Keeping his palms against the clammy walls, he crept forward. As he descended, the air took on the rank odor of sulfur, but at least it grew warmer. At length, the passage made a turn, and the slave stopped, blinking as light flared in the granite walls. He had reached the heart of the mound.

It was a treasure chamber, and scattered all around was the wealth of a mighty, unknown tribe. Serpentine arm rings of gold lay on the floor beside brooches of silver filigree, iron swords with gilded hilts, bowls of rare, red Samian ware, hammer-shaped amulets that bore the staring eyes of the old god Thor, and glittering coins. The man stepped forward and then froze in his tracks. He was not the first to find the treasure. Curved around the chamber, keeping a jealous watch already centuries old, was a dragon. In the course of its wanderings, it had discovered the treasure, hidden by the vanquished tribe's last survivor, and – as was the habit of dragons – had set itself to guard the gold.

It crouched on clawed feet in enormous coils, its scaled sides gleaming. But the leathery wings were folded and the long head rested on the floor of the chamber, hooded membranes closed over ancient eyes. Smoke curled from the blackened nostrils, and as the slave watched, the dragon exhaled a narrow ribbon of flame. The beast was the source of the chamber's heat and light.

Seeing that the creature slept soundly, the man acted: He snatched from the hoard a golden cup, a peace offering for his master. (His craving for freedom was much faded by now, and thoughts of food and drink had grown vivid.) Then he turned and made his way hastily up through the chill darkness of the corridor, into the cold air outside. Like a wild thing pursued, he ran from that place, never stopping until, hours later, he was safe within the walls of his settlement. He got a beating for his pains. But his master took the golden cup.

That slave proved the bane of his people, for he had disturbed the guardian of the treasure. All-seeing and all-knowing, the dragon awoke and recognized its loss. It recognized, too, the mortal smell. Slowly it dragged its heavy coils up through the corridor that led to its lair, and in the dying light, it searched the waste around the barrow, the massive head lowered as it traced the mortal path. It found the direction and, with a shriek and a spurt of flame, took to the air, soaring on great wings toward the kingdom of the Geats.

Over every settlement it flew, and the noise of its screaming brought the people from their houses, white faces turned toward the sky. High above them, beneath the canopy of stars, the dragon caracoled in a dance of death, howling its dragon song as it began its descent.

Its strikes were terrible and swift: Spewing gouts of flame, it sailed over the roofs of the houses and disappeared into the distance. In that land, all dwellings – even royal halls – were made of wood, wattle and daub, and thatch, and these materials were tinder for the dragon's flame. Throughout the Geatish kingdom, the night grew bright as the settlements blazed high, like so many funeral pyres.

The dragon spared nothing. When at last morning came, the Geatish settlements were charred ruins, covered with a pall of smoke and echoing with the wailing laments of the women.

In the midst of this, the warriors of the kingdom gathered in council with their leader. He was a man long famous in the songs of the bards. His name was Beowulf, who years before had slain the monster Grendel and the monster's loathsome dam, and thus delivered an entire people from destruction.

But that was in another country. Beowulf was old now, having ruled the Geats for fifty years. Still, shaggy and gray as he had grown, he towered above his fellows. Beowulf was not only the King but also the champion of his people. Only he, said the King to his assembled warriors, could slay the dragon.

Accordingly, armored in gold and bearing an iron shield to protect him from the dragon's fiery breath, Beowulf set out for the beast's lair. He was accompanied by eleven princelings, sturdy warriors all. They dragged with them the wretched slave to show the way.

The company came at last to the headland where the dragon laired, and there they paused while Beowulf rested. All was peaceful; no sign of life came from the rocky barrow. The King spoke sadly to his companions; he felt, it was later said, a premonition of doom. He ordered the men to stand at a distance. Then he strode with firm steps across the flattened grass to the barrow entrance.

Raising the shield, the old man roared out his challenge, a loud battle cry that echoed against the stones and reverberated in the air around the dragon's den. The sound died away into silence. The watching men shifted nervously, but the King stood immobile.

Without warning, a mass of smoke, shot with flame, burst from the portal of the barrow. It was followed instantly by the dragon, bent like a serrated bow, massively clawed and fanged, spewing fire and molten spittle. The King's companions backed away and sought shelter—to their eternal shame, for those who told the tale never forgot to mention how they quailed at this moment. But Beowulf held his ground. He raised high his broadsword and brought it down on the beast in a lightning swing.

The sword did not bite. It glanced harmlessly off the dragon's scales. The beast spat fire around the King, blackening his skin and setting his hair aflame. Yet the old man stood immovable, heedless of the flame and pain.

Unable to bear the sight, one companion returned to the King's side. His name was Wiglaf; crying devotion and defiance, he plunged into the smoke beside his lord as the dragon belched fire once more. Beowulf raised the sword a second time and swung savagely at the creature's head. The blade struck the bony skull and shivered to splinters in his hand, and the King was left defenseless, clutching a useless hilt.

At once, the dragon closed in. With gleaming fangs, it slashed at the King's throat, tearing the flesh open. Almost at the same instant, Wiglaf thrust his sword up into the folds of unarmored skin below the beast's jaw. The huge head swung slowly from side to side, and the wings arched awkwardly as the dragon recoiled. Struggling in a welter of smoke and slime, the two men again and again struck at the dragon, Beowulf with a dagger from his belt, Wiglaf with his sword. Then the ground shook as the beast fell, a mess of stinking blood and boiling viscera.

Suddenly there was silence. The King staggered, falling to his knees and then to the ground. Wiglaf knelt beside him, eased his golden helmet off and bent to catch the old one's words. Then he disappeared into the dragon's lair. Moments later, he emerged again, bearing an armload of serpentine torques and jeweled swords. These he dropped beside the King and knelt again to hear whispered orders. By now, the others had gathered around.

Wiglaf, glancing up at them with contempt written clear on his face, jerked his head toward the smoking body of the dragon. "Give it to the sea," he said curtly.

And so, sweating and cursing, the companions dragged the bloody carcass to the verge of the headland and pushed it over. It fell down the cliffside in writhing coils and aimlessly flapping wings, until it struck rock and at last, broken, plunged into the foaming waters. A black stain spread there and lapped against the rocks, but that, too, was shortly washed away.

They returned to the King, in time to see the old man's last movement. Poisoned by the dragon venom, he was dying. He took the golden collar from his own neck and put it on Wiglaf's. Then the light in the old eyes faded.

The princelings honored the dead King in the manner that Wiglaf – following his lord's instructions – told them. They bore him on his iron shield to the place of burning, and they made a splendid pyre, hung with the helmets, shields and shining corselets that he had worn. The funeral flames roared around him, and the body crumbled to ashes.

Beowulf's people built a second stone barrow on the dragon's headland, as the King had asked. It was so enormous that it could be seen by sailors far at sea. In the barrow they left the dragon's hoard, and there the treasure stayed, as precious and useless to humankind as it had been to the dragon. Poets kept Beowulf's name alive in mourning. They called him "the gentlest and most gracious of men, the

A perilous feasting place

The naturalists of Europe, speculating about dragons, wrote of a wonderful tree called the perindeus, which grew in India. The tree's sweet fruit drew flocks of doves. Dragons, which had a particular fondness for the taste of doves, lurked nearby – but not too near, for even the shadow of the tree was poison to them. When doves left the tree's protective embrace, however, they were likely to fall victim to the serpents' swift strikes.

kindest to his people and the most desirous of renown."

His end suited a life so full of valor. The Geatish King had fought against one of humankind's oldest enemies, standing up to its cruel strength with no thought of the inequality of the match. Such a deed was not unique, of course. Beowulf's last battle was repeated many times during the long centuries when dragons trod the earth. These evil engines of destruction had to be killed, it seemed, if civilization was to survive and prosper.

But nothing about dragon lore is simple: Terrible in their fierceness, dragons were the dreaded foe of men; at the same time, they were often idolized by men for their power. The dragons of Europe – fire-breathing, water-poisoning and predatory – were almost universally regarded as a scourge, a source of plague and starvation and violent death. The dragons of Asia, on the other hand, were powerful and on the whole beneficent creatures, bearers of rain and the growth it encouraged. Some were worshipped as gods, and many a noble Asian line proudly claimed the distinction of dragon blood.

Whether European or Asian, the race of dragons was as old as creation and as varied as nature itself. Their very characteristics were difficult to classify or define. The accounts of chroniclers and scholars from the centuries of the dragons' ascendancy agree only on a general picture of a serpentine beast protected by a body armor of overlapping scales and equipped with claws to cut, teeth to tear, and breath and blood to burn. The creatures almost always had preternaturally acute vision; in-

deed, "dragon" seems to have been derived from the ancient Greek verb "to see." A few had both this keen eyesight and, for their prey, a burning basilisk gaze that was death to behold.

In other particulars, however, the accounts of dragons reveal a bewildering range of sizes and forms. Most dragons seem to have been about twenty feet long, but a few, paragons of the breed, were said to have reached lengths of 140 cubits – 210 feet. Some of them had legs, others had wings, and many had both or neither. There were dragons with not one but seven or even a hundred heads; with not one but three rows of deadly teeth. Their blood was thought to be poison, but it – along with other parts of their anatomies – was used in medicinal cures and magic potions. The foulness of their breath – reeking of fire and brimstone, of drying blood and decaying flesh – was legendary, but some dragons scorched with fire and others breathed pestilence.

All dragons seemed linked with elemental and chaotic powers, and in the Near East and Europe at least, these powers were almost exclusively destructive: The dragon race maintained a dangerous opposition to the human one. The human enemy, thinking perhaps to acquire something of the dragons' might, adopted dragon images for themselves as aids to battle all through the years of the dragons' rule. Persian soldiers took the field carrying before them immense dragon figures as a means of frightening opposing armies; the Romans, following a similar practice,

painted red dragons on their battle standards and called the standards *dracones*, or dragons. In their triumphal parades, they flew a kind of dragon kite—an image made with an open mouth that caught the wind and hissed ferociously.

Warring Celtic and Teutonic tribes all claimed the dragon as their symbol. Among Anglo-Saxons, the feat of slaying a chief was expressed as slaying a dragon. The berserkers—those half-mad warriors of ancient Scandinavia—named their warships dragon barques and ornamented the prows with dragon heads, devices to intimidate their enemies. This honoring of the dragons' power would change. The time would come—as the world aged, human societies spread and grew strong, and men imposed their own order on nature—when dragons would be pushed farther and farther from civilization, so that on maps the last wildernesses were marked with the simple warning, "Here be dragons." The time would come when mortal heroes—not only warriors, but saints and even children—would conquer the dragons who ventured among them, and the last of that mighty race would disappear.

But that time was centuries in arriving, for in the young age of the world, mortals had few weapons that would avail against dragons. Rulers of wind and fire and water, the great beasts possessed an ancient intelligence—an innate magic—born of the primal powers from which they sprang. Dragons, unlike men, were creatures of chaos, formed at the very creation of the world.

Or so mortals said. When they spoke of beginnings and first things, they talked of dragons; when they spoke of the order imposed on primal disorder, they talked of dragon fights. The Norsemen of Beowulf's time, for instance, described the universe in terms of a giant ash tree, Yggdrasil, whose trunk and branches supported all the orders of existence, and whose roots reached into the worlds of the gods, of men and of the dead. Trapped among the roots of Yggdrasil forever, gnawing eternally at them and thus at the foundation of ordered existence, was the dragon Nidhoggr, the Dread Biter, the first dragon.

And ringing the mortal world—called Midgard—was another mighty serpent. The child of a god imprisoned in the abyss at the beginning of time, its name was Jormungandr, and it lay hidden in the icy depths of the ocean that embraced mortal lands. The chroniclers said that the thunder god, Thor, drew the beast from the waters once and fought him, but to no avail. The dragon remained on the ocean floor, and the only signs of its presence were the turmoil and storms caused by its writhing. But the Norsemen believed that Thor and the serpent were destined to fight once more, at

Destroyer at the roots of the world

According to Norse belief, an immense, unseen tree called Yggdrasil stretched from the vault of heaven to the depths of hell. A dragon named Nidhoggr gnawed perpetually at the roots, seeking to destroy the order of creation, but the order had a battalion of defenders. Three godlike beings called Norns sat calmly near the dragon at the roots, spinning the threads of mortal fate. Stags browsed at the tree and watered the earth with dew from their antlers. A goat that chewed the tree's bark provided mead as milk for mortal heroes who would rid the world of the dragon race. Of the birds that perched in Yggdrasil's branches, the greatest was the eagle—a steadfast dragon enemy that sang forever of creation and destruction.

Ragnarök — World's End. Then, in the midst of perpetual winter, when the heavens split asunder and chaos returned, Thor would kill the serpent as it sprang from the waters. The dragon's dying breath would slay the god; and in sheets of fire, the world itself would die, scattering into the elements from which it had come.

The coming of order — the division of light from darkness, of the heavens and the earth from the waters — required that the first dragons be conquered, since they were demons of disorder. Their foes were gods, not men, for these leviathans existed long before humankind appeared.

Poets of every ancient land spoke of the titanic patterns of their conflicts. From the fertile crescent of Mesopotamia, formed by the Tigris and Euphrates Rivers, came the earliest tales. There, thousands of years ago, an unknown scribe in the land of Babylon set down on seven clay tablets a story of creation that had already descended through generations of his people by word of mouth.

In the beginning, wrote the scribe, when all was dark and formless, two primal beings came into existence. One was male, the spirit of fresh water and the void, and it was called Apsu. The other was female, the spirit of salt water and chaos, and it was a dragon, composed of elements of dangerous creatures yet to come: It possessed the jaws of a crocodile, the teeth of a lion, the wings of a bat, the legs of a lizard, the talons of an eagle, the body of a python, the horns of a bull. The dragon's name was Tiamat.

The union of these two creatures, wrote the scribe, spawned the gods, and one of

them killed his father, Apsu. Then, in her dragon's fury, Tiamat gave birth to a new kind of offspring, a menagerie of monsters to afflict her first brood. She brought forth scorpion men and demon lions, giant serpents and — lesser versions of herself — glittering dragons. Chaos reigned in the formless void.

In order to defend themselves, the gods called one of their own number as a champion. This was Marduk, who would become lord of the universe. Armed with a net and a club, with poison, with bow and arrow and a quiver of lightning bolts, the god Marduk mounted a storm chariot drawn by four swift and violent steeds. He was escorted by the four winds and a mighty hurricane.

Thus arrayed in terror, Marduk searched the universe for Tiamat, his dragon mother. He spread his net across the void and caught her in it, and he let fly the winds in her face until they filled and distended her body and she could no longer close her mouth. Then, taking aim with his bow, Marduk shot an arrow between Tiamat's open jaws, straight down into her heart.

"Her inner parts he cleft," wrote the scribe. "He split her heart. He rendered her powerless and destroyed her life. He felled her body and stood upright on it."

The death of Tiamat threw her beast-brood into confusion, and they fled for their lives. But Marduk caught them all in his net and put them in chains and threw them into the infernal regions. Then he disposed of Tiamat's own monstrous car-

Using a chain baited with the head of an ox, the Norse god Thor hauled the Midgard
serpent from the sea while the father god, Odin, watched from on high. Thor raised his hammer
to kill the beast, but the chain snapped and the dragon escaped.

Babylonian priests wrote that, before light separated from darkness and time began, the god
Marduk slew his dragon forebear Tiamat, enemy of order. In the depths of the void,
Marduk pursued and caught Tiamat, and he split her great body asunder.

Across the Egyptian skies each day sailed the sun god Ra, his barque a burnished throne. The chants of his hyena-faced guard, Seth, held off the dragon Apep, who ruled over darkness and sought to devour the god of light.

cass. He split her skull and severed her arteries; he cleft her body "like a fish into its two parts," from one of which he fashioned the firmament and from the other the solid earth.

He constructed a great dwelling place for the gods in the heavens and installed the stars and the moon, the keeper of time. And with the blood of one of Tiamat's monster brood, Marduk manufactured human beings to serve the gods, "in order that the gods should live in a world to rejoice their hearts."

Thus — in the eldest terms — was the world wrought from the disorder of the cosmos. Almost the same creation tale was told in lands as far from Babylon as India and Denmark. In Babylon, the story of the slaying of the first dragon was read each year, to remind the people of their origin and that of the world they lived in, and

to celebrate the triumph of the first dragonslayer over the creature of darkness.

The people had reason to celebrate order: All around them in their sun-washed region were growing the glories that order brought. Great cities flourished there: Babylon itself, graced with wondrous gardens; Ur, with its towering ziggurat; high-walled Nineveh, shielded and ornamented by a gate of marvelous beasts. Nor was high civilization confined to Mesopotamia. To the northwest, the red-columned palace cities of Crete's Minoan kings reared proudly over the Aegean Sea. To the west, at Memphis, rose the palaces of the pharoahs and the gold stone pyramids that sheltered their dead.

Yet all these proud monuments were but frail reeds, easily broken by the winds of change and the dangers of the surrounding wilderness. Life was short and

the times uncertain. Conquering armies swept into the rich realms, famine and plague sometimes raged through the cities, and the earth itself—still young and sometimes trembling—betrayed the small folk who lived on its surface.

As the centuries passed, the cities fell and the sands of desert wastes drifted over their toppled stones. Wolves howled in the empty streets. It is no wonder that in the roaring of the four winds and the crackle of lightning, in the belching fires of volcanoes and the cataclysmic shiftings of the ground, mortals saw chaos threaten again, and they heard the dragon's scream.

They heard it behind everything that endangered order—even, in Egypt, in the alternation of day and night, which the Egyptians described as the voyage of their sun god, Ra.

Sovereign lord of the sky, Ra boarded his day boat every dawn and was rowed from east to west across the heavens by a crew of gods and the souls of the blessed dead. Each dawn, the people of Egypt watched Ra's barque rise like a golden discus flung over the horizon of the eastern desert and lift slowly above the worn ridges of Sinai and the green fields of the Nile flood plains, adding brilliance to height as it arced upward toward its noonday apogee.

There the barque hung over river and city with an intensity so fierce that not even the temple priests could bear to lift up their eyes to their god. Every living thing took refuge from its scorching rays— the sailors of the river feluccas under their deck awnings, the laborers in the fields under the clacking palms, the lions in the tall grasses of the plains, the crocodiles in the dank gloom of the papyrus swamps.

At noon nothing stirred in ancient Egypt, and Ra shone white-hot in the full power and vigor of his diurnal youth, an affirmation of life and growth and order.

But Ra had a mortal enemy – Apep, dragon of the depths of the celestial Nile and lord of the underworld. To mount the skies, the sun god had to battle and defeat the dragon, and not once, as Marduk defeated Tiamat, but once each day.

Every evening, when Ra reached the western horizon, when the hot desert dusk flared through shades of lilac and oleander and the water birds came winging to roost in vast flocks across the darkening Nile, the sun god on his night boat floated beneath the earth and through the realm of the dead, where the dragon Apep ruled and where his strength was greatest. As the light faded, people whispered of the perils of the underworld where their god traveled. The gates were said to be guarded by riddling demons whose mysterious questions had to be answered correctly before the sun god could pass.

Then the barque glided from dark cavern to dark cavern, towed by a team of cobras and jackals, and each cavern that Ra entered grew bright with his radiance; the dead awoke to momentary life before surrendering again to the agony of darkness; and the forces of chaos, chief among them Apep, gathered to attack their light-bringing enemy.

Every night Apep tried to destroy Ra, and every night Ra was saved by a celestial crew led by a hyena-faced storm god called Seth. And each dawn, Apep was defeated, trapped by the spirits of the reddening sky, decapitated by Seth and hacked into pieces. Every day the dragon's dismembered body was reconstituted and made whole again and the cycle of conflict was repeated. Thus, in the struggle between these two opposed but complementary powers, Apep and Ra, the equilibrium of the universe was preserved, and every new dawn was a victory of light over darkness, order over chaos.

Or so the Egyptians said, in dim remembrance of the dreaming era at the beginning of the world. In that age before the race of dragons stalked freely on the young earth, their only enemies were the gods who fathered humankind.

The traces of those ancient battles were everywhere to be seen. The seafaring Greeks in the time of Homer, for instance, observed the islands of the Cyclades scattered like pearls across the lapis blue Aegean, saw the ruins of once-mighty Crete, heard the rumbling of Sicilia's smoldering volcano, Mount Etna, and sang of the monster Typhon.

Last of the Titans, those omnipotent first gods of Greece, Typhon was the son of Ge and Tartarus – the Earth and the Underworld. He was a vicious and implacable foe of the Olympian gods, deities of the second generation, who one day would overthrow the Titans and reign in their place.

Ge kept her creature concealed as long as she could, the Greeks said, but the time came at last when Typhon burst from his hiding place in Asia Minor and, raging with blood lust, strode toward Greece and Mount Olympus, bent on destroying the young race of gods who threatened his own.

He was a horror to behold. His height was such that he towered above the mountains and could wade through the sea. He was composed of a miscellany of parts, more hideous for their meaningless conjunction. He had a hundred dragon heads, each with burning eyes and an insanely gaping mouth that spat fire and vomited rocks, each with a voice that gibbered and bellowed the screams of a damned thing. The torso was human flesh, but beneath it were glistening coils—a writhing, spinning mass of serpents.

A true son of chaos, Typhon took storm and destruction with him; the word "typhoon," in fact, derives from his name. He strode through the Aegean, tossing the clustered Cyclades about like stones. His fiery breath touched the lovely, forested island of Thera, and its western half exploded, leaving the island a barren, blackened crescent. The earthquakes and the tidal waves caused by the explosion overwhelmed the kingdom of Minos on Crete: On a single day of water and fire and smoke, the proud red palaces were reduced to rubble.

It was said that the Olympians fled before the creature's wrath—all, that is, but Zeus, the mightiest of the young gods. With strength and cunning, with a sickle of adamant and a quiver of thunderbolts, Zeus fought the dragon in a battle that raged across Greece into Syria, where—so the storytellers say—great furrows gouged by Typhon became the beds of the rivers.

At last, however, Zeus drove the monster north into the Ionian Sea and thence to the shallows off the Italian coast. There Typhon fell, heads writhing and spewing, and the young god wrenched an island from the sea and flung it upon the monster. That, according to the chroniclers, was Sicilia, and the swelling ground that covered Typhon was Mount Etna. But the

A pallet worthy of a god

All across the ancient world, people spoke of dragons when they spoke of first things — and India was no exception. Holy men of that land said that the world was supported by Sesha, an eleven-headed serpentine creature whose title was Ananta, meaning the Endless One. Far from being an agent of disorder, as most dragons were, Ananta served Vishnu, the Lord of the Universe, offering its long back as a couch when the god chose to sleep.

21

dragon lived on. Sometimes, in his rages, he let forth a blast from his hundred mouths, spitting molten bile over the farms and vineyards of the humans who came to dwell unknowing upon his tomb.

Tales of Typhon and his kind, however, were told long centuries after the world was formed, by people who could not possibly have seen the monsters. The stories helped in understanding the mystery of how things came into being. They served, too, as a kind of reason for the presence of the frightening creatures that continued to share the earth with men.

Sleepless guardian of the golden apples

In Greece, poets told this tale: At the end of the world lay an island called the Gardens of Ocean, and on the island grew a tree that bore golden apples. Because a bite of the apples' flesh would give a mortal the knowledge rightfully possessed by immortals, the gods had set the never-sleeping dragon Ladon to guard the tree.

A mortal King sent the hero Hercules to find and steal the golden apples. Some storytellers said that the hero slew the many-headed monster and stole a branch of the tree, but others insisted that no mortal – not even a hero – could survive an encounter with Ladon. Instead, they claimed, Hercules persuaded the god Atlas – on whose shoulders rested the heavens – to travel to the enchanted gardens and pluck the magical fruit. While Atlas was away on this mission, Hercules assumed the god's role: The mortal stood on a mountaintop and held up the sky until its proper pillar returned with the apples.

For the first dragons left descendants in the world. The dragons that laired not far from human habitations — in rivers and caves, on mountains and in windy wildernesses — were not the leviathans of the legends. All the same, they struck terror in the human heart. They carried in them

some of the powers of their cosmic ancestors — in their size, in their ferocity and devouring appetites, in their capacity for flight. And they also embodied some of the elements of the chaos from which they sprang. The earthly dragons that mortals knew were creatures of wind and water and storm, and like those capricious, elemental entities, they had a shifting quality alien to the ordered patterns of human civilizations. Though clearly animal, many dragons could speak; though reptilian, they flew. Many of them could assume the cloak of invisibility; many of them could alter their own shapes; many breathed fire.

The creatures' monstrous strength and ferocity were such that in classical times they were said to be predators of that other natural behemoth, the elephant: In Ethiopia, it was reported, dragons were called simply, elephant killers. Pliny the Elder, a Roman of infinite curiosity, speculated in his studies of natural phenomena that dragons hunted elephants to drink their blood — which was known for its remarkable coolness — and thus find relief from the heat of the desert and of their own bodies.

The dragon, wrote the Roman scholar, lies "coiled up and concealed in the river, in wait for the elephants when they come to drink, upon which it darts out, fastens itself around an elephant's trunk, and then fixes its teeth behind the ear, that being the only place which the elephant cannot protect with the trunk. The dragons, it is said, are of such vast size that they can swallow the whole of the blood; consequently, the elephant, being drained of its blood, falls to the ground, exhausted, while the dragon, intoxicated with the draught, is crushed beneath it and so shares its fate."

The dragons that lingered long into the time of men, however, were not merely predators. Dragons frequently served as guardians. It is not surprising, considering that they were elemental creatures, that dragons guarded water – rivers and springs. It is less explicable that a fair number of dragons – like the firedrake that Beowulf slew – kept watch over treasures. Yet gold and silver are elements as old as the earth, and such precious stones as rubies and emeralds and sapphires were formed by the earth's slow, internal workings. Perhaps dragons, ancient as all of these treasures, had perforce to protect the relics of the unformed cosmos.

In any case, their guardianships drew the attention of humankind: The rise of the dragonslayer was the result not only of the need for humans to protect themselves and their own, but also of the value humans placed on metals and jewels in the dragon's possession.

Some of these were fabled. The Greeks told often of the golden apples of the Hesperides, who were the daughters of Atlas, the god who held the sky on his shoulders. The apples grew on a single tree in the Gardens of Ocean at the western end of the world, and they were guarded by a spawn of Typhon himself, a many-headed monster who never slept but coiled himself perpetually around the base of the tree, cherishing the gleaming ap-

ples. It became one of the twelve labors of the hero Hercules to steal the precious fruit, whose flesh was said to hold the secrets of knowledge and of immortality. The hero – whose own shield was emblazoned with a coiled dragon, its eyes aglow with battle fury – slew the dragon, some said, and so gained the apples.

And a loathsome, thousand-coiled dragon lived once in a grove at Colchis, on the Black Sea, forever protecting the curls of the golden fleece. The fleece, the relic of a magical ram that could fly, think and talk, was eventually stolen by the Greek adventurer Jason, who lulled the guardian to sleep with a magic potion.

Another Greek tale, however, tells not of gold but of something more valuable to humanity. This tale begins in Phoenicia, a land of rich traders that lay along the eastern shore of the Mediterranean Sea. It happened that the daughter of the country's King disappeared, and the King sent his son, Cadmus of Tyre, to travel the world in search of her. This the young man did. Sailing west with stout companions in the black ships of his country, Cadmus searched the islands of the Aegean and the coast of Greece, but he found no sign of the girl.

He was valiant, but he had failed, and he was afraid to return to his father. Instead, Cadmus led his small company of men to the oracle at Delphi, high in the mountains of the north, where the priestess of Apollo gave her predictions. He sought the oracle's guidance as to the course he should follow.

In the cold Delphian cave, buried among the pines of the mountain, Cadmus

An enchantress' shifting of the odds

A young warrior named Jason, son of a King of Thessaly, outwitted a dragon once and retrieved the treasure it guarded. His feat happened this way:

At the urging of his uncle, Jason embarked on a quest to obtain the fleece of a fabulous golden ram that had been sacrificed years before in the kingdom of Colchis on the shores of the Black Sea. The fleece was guarded by a dragon that never slept. Jason sailed to Colchis with a company of the heroes of Greece – Hercules, Theseus and Orpheus among them.

When the men arrived, they found the Colchian King, Aeetes, reluctant to give up his treasure; he consented only on the terms that Jason sow a collection of dragon's teeth in the earth. As the King well knew, those teeth would spring from the ground as warriors and fall upon Jason.

But the King's plans were foiled by his daughter, Medea, a sorceress of great power. She desired Jason, and he promised her marriage in exchange for her aid. This she gave: When Jason sowed the teeth in the ground, they did indeed spring up as fierce warriors; but Jason threw Medea's magic stone among them, and they fell upon one another, not on him. After that slaughter, he approached the guardian dragon, armed with a charmed distillation that irresistibly induced sleep. As the beast slumbered, he made off with the fleece. Then, taking Medea along, he returned to Thessaly in triumph.

25

found the priestess seated on her golden tripod, her hair floating wildly about her face and her eyes closed in the Delphic trance. He told his tale and asked what he should do. The answer was only hoarse moaning, followed by the chant of the attendant priest, who interpreted the meaningless syllables the priestess uttered.

The oracle was never straightforward. Cadmus was told that outside the cave he would find a cow, a sacred animal in Greece at that time. He and his company were to follow the cow wherever the beast went, until it lay down. In the place where the cow halted, said the priest, the Phoenician should establish a city and rule it for himself. Cadmus obeyed.

All happened as the priest said. The cow was indeed waiting in the road outside the cave. Cadmus and his companions followed it for many days as it ambled slowly south, until at last it lay down at a place on the broad, green plain of Panope, near a grove that echoed with the bubbling of a spring. The men threw themselves to the grass and rested. After some time, Cadmus sent them into the grove to draw water from the spring.

Another hero of Greece was Cadmus, who braved a dragon's jaws to slay the beast with a spear.
In the wilderness where the dragon had held sway, Cadmus built the mighty city of Thebes.

An hour passed and then another. The men did not return. At length, the young man rose, gathered his weapons and entered the wood in search of them. He walked among the trees until he found the spring – and more than the spring. The ground was covered with dead men – his Tyrian companions, torn and bloodied, their sightless eyes staring at the branches above. Swaying over them, crested head erect, eyes flaming, golden scales gleaming, was a dragon. Blood dripped from its triple rows of teeth; shreds of flesh clung to its curving claws. Its body was taut and swollen with venom, and a fearful stench drifted over the carnage. The beast saw the young man and bared its teeth, crouching for the kill.

But Cadmus was quicker. He hurled a javelin straight at the creature. The frail weapon slid between the scales and penetrated the flesh. The dragon gave a grating hiss and twisted its head, biting savagely at the shaft. Bloody flecks of foam appeared at its mouth, and smoke shot from its nostrils.

With a vicious twist, the dragon uncoiled and advanced toward the warrior. The ground shook. Cadmus retreated, step by step, holding his spear braced against his belly and pointed at the creature. Like a cat or a snake, the head advanced, snapping at the iron spear point. It missed, and snapped again.

When he could retreat no farther and the foul, burning breath was beginning to overcome him, Cadmus let the animal's teeth meet on the spear, and at that moment he thrust, straight and deep into the dragon's gut.

The dragon spurted black blood and smoke; it lurched back among the trees, howling, while Cadmus of Tyre, gasping and sweating, watched. The dragon staggered against a tree. The coils twisted convulsively, the great sides heaved and then, at last, they were still.

A curious thing happened next, something the oracle had not foretold. Cadmus walked past the bodies of his comrades to the body of the dragon. With a foot, he nudged the golden scales. The creature made no move, but a voice sounded in the young man's head.

"Sow the teeth," it said, "and you shall reap wonders."

He stared at the dragon, but the dragon was motionless, the flames in its eyes burned out. He nudged it once more, and again he heard the voice.

"Sow, mortal," it repeated. "If you would reap, then you must sow."

With a shrug, he knelt down, breathing through his mouth to avoid the terrible stench. He touched the jaw, and it fell open. Then, with his knife, Cadmus set to work. He pried the great teeth, one by one, from the still-warm jaw and dropped them on the ground. It was a sickening and bloody business, but the grisly job was done at last. He rested for a while, then gathered the teeth and took them out of that charnel house of a wood.

In the soft ground of the plain, Cadmus dug a shallow furrow, and into it he threw the teeth of the golden dragon. He covered them with clods of earth and turned

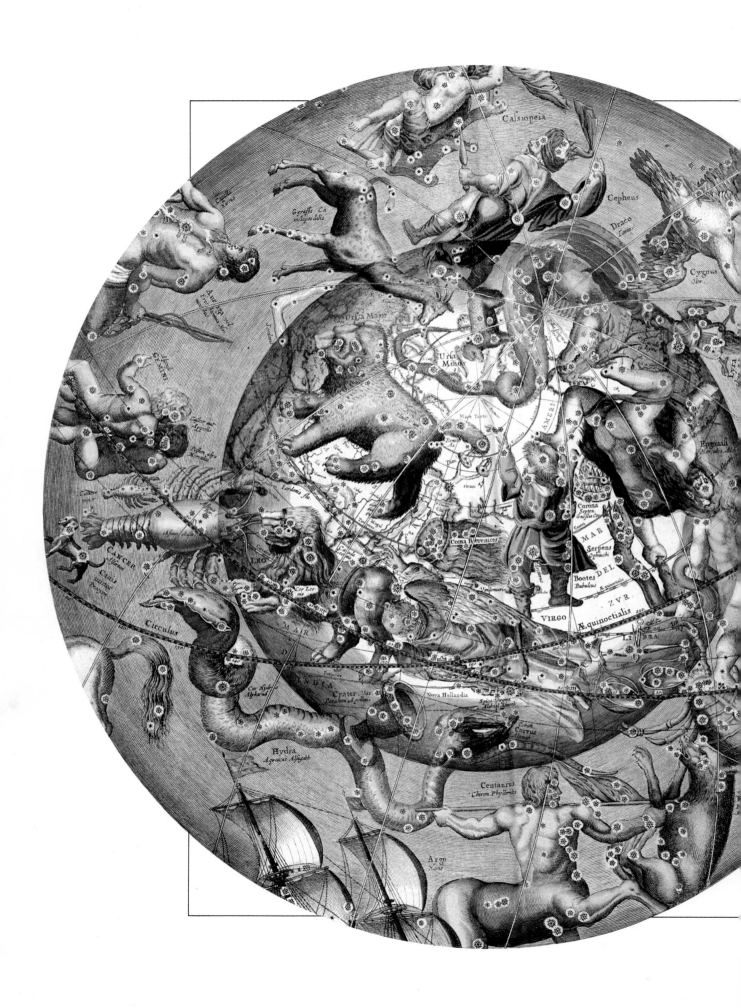

wearily back to the wood, to bury what was left of his young companions.

He had gone no more than twenty paces when he heard a rustle behind him. Cadmus whipped around at once. The ground quivered, the clods of earth bounced, and something glittered in the dirt. Throughout the field winked tiny candle flames of gold. The flames rose higher: They were spear points and they were followed by spear shafts, and then by the nodding plumes of helmets, and then by helmets themselves. Silently rising from the ground was a crop of full-grown warriors. As soon as each was free of the dirt, he breathed and turned to his fellow and spoke. Cadmus stepped forward, ready to fight until he died, but the warriors waved him aside. "This is our war and no affair of yours," a deep voice cried. And the soldiers set upon one another, thrusting and stabbing without a sound. One by one they fell, all through the afternoon while the mysterious battle of unknown enemies went on. As the warriors fell, they sank into the earth without a trace. At last, only five of that great company were left, and one of these five spoke. "We must end this carnage, brothers, and make a new fate," said the man, and he threw his weapons down. The others followed him. The five young warriors turned as one to Cadmus and offered their hearts and hands.

Together, then, the young men worked in peace. They buried the companions of Cadmus. They heaved the deflated, mutilated dragon body into the air. Surprisingly, instead of tangling in the tree branches, it soared off, light as mist, higher and higher until it became a mere speck in the blue. No one knew where it went, but later generations said that the constellation Draco, coiling among the stars, was Cadmus' dragon.

The men camped that night, and the next morning gathered in council. In the years that followed, they built a great city on the plain. The city they built was Thebes—a mighty fortress that Cadmus ruled for years, and a center of learning: Cadmus, it was said, brought to Greece the alphabet of letters that the Phoenicians of his homeland had invented.

Thus, the process of the first creation was echoed in the world of mortals: The slaying of the creatures of chaos made possible the establishment of order and of the growing powers of humankind. The beginning of the end of the mighty race of dragons had begun.

Yet the fate of Western dragons lay not in the emergent role of man-as-dragonslayer—a development that may have quickened the end but was hardly its cause. Rather, the end was brought about by the dragon's own diminishment—the long, slow slide that reduced the dragon, by stages, from a creature filling the void and towering above creation to a beast that could be bested by a man armed with nothing more than bravery, daring and a strong weapon. ᕲᐢ

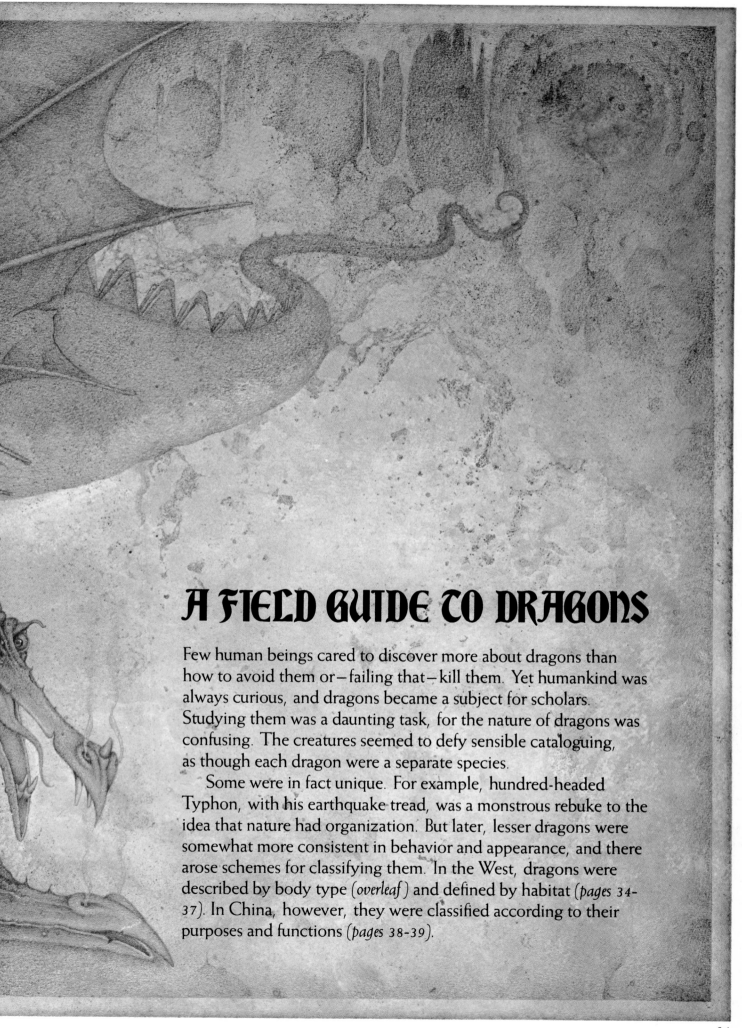

A FIELD GUIDE TO DRAGONS

Few human beings cared to discover more about dragons than how to avoid them or—failing that—kill them. Yet humankind was always curious, and dragons became a subject for scholars. Studying them was a daunting task, for the nature of dragons was confusing. The creatures seemed to defy sensible cataloguing, as though each dragon were a separate species.

Some were in fact unique. For example, hundred-headed Typhon, with his earthquake tread, was a monstrous rebuke to the idea that nature had organization. But later, lesser dragons were somewhat more consistent in behavior and appearance, and there arose schemes for classifying them. In the West, dragons were described by body type (*overleaf*) and defined by habitat (*pages 34-37*). In China, however, they were classified according to their purposes and functions (*pages 38-39*).

The Array of Classical Forms

The amphiptère

A legless, winged serpent, the amphiptère could be found along the banks of the Nile and in Arabia, where it guarded frankincense-bearing trees and threatened all who would harvest the precious resin.

The wyvern

Feared for its viciousness and for the pestilence it brought to northern Europe, Greece and Ethiopia, the wyvern had a coiling trunk that bore a pair of eagle's legs, which were tucked beneath its wings. The name derived from the Saxon word *wivere*, or "serpent."

The heraldic dragon

The most widespread and formidable of its kind, the heraldic dragon had massive fangs, four clawed legs and a ridge of sharp spines that stretched from its spiked nose to its barbed and stinging tail.

The guivre

The legless and wingless guivre would have seemed a mere serpent, albeit an immensely powerful one, except for its massive dragon head, horned and bearded. Guivres liked to live in forests and wells – anywhere near water.

The lindworm

Falling between the birdlike wyvern and the snakelike guivre, the lindworm had a serpentine body with one pair of legs. It was flightless. The Italian traveler Marco Polo reported seeing some lindworms while crossing the steppes of Central Asia.

A Diversity of Habitats

Cave dwellers

Wherever caves existed, there were likely to be dragons, whose serpent nature found comfort in dank, cold darkness. Such lairs were private and easily guarded, thus suited to these solitary, suspicious beasts; caves close to towns were particularly desirable, because they were convenient to food.

Mountain predators

Craggy or cave-riddled mountains provided impregnable aeries for keen-eyed, winged dragons. These beasts, like falcons, could spy their prey from on high, rocket down for the kill and return to their dens to feed unmolested. Among the most dangerous of such mountain dwellers was the fire-breathing *Tatzlwurm*, which fed upon the stray cattle and lost children of Alpine Switzerland and Austria.

Aquatic denizens

The primal element, water, sheltered dragons, who were the primal beasts. They inhabited seas and rivers and lakes all over the world. Such places offered boat traffic and fish to prey on; but more than that, they provided a watery cloak that allowed dragons to approach river towns and seaports undetected.

Swamp beasts

Marshes, like caves, made
havens for dragons. The
English called swamp dragons
"knuckers," and the dragons'
retreats, reputed to be bot-
tomless, were knucker holes.
These were small, deep
pits that were cold in summer,
never frozen in winter and
that gave off an eerie vapor.

Cosmic Division of Labor

Celestial guardians

The celestial dragons of China protected the heavens, supporting the mansions of the gods and shielding them from decay. Only these dragons – and their earthly likenesses on the imperial regalia – had five claws. All other dragons had only three or four.

Treasure keepers

Subterranean dragons had charge of all the precious jewels and metals buried in the earth. Each of these dragons bore an enormous pearl that was reputed to multiply whatever it touched; the pearl symbolized another hidden treasure, wisdom.

Weathermakers

Floating across the sky, a changeable blue in color, spiritual dragons governed the wind, clouds and rain on which life has always depended. The Chinese took care to appease them, for if these weatherworkers grew angry or neglectful, the result was certain disaster.

River lords

Earth dragons determined the courses of rivers, regulated their flow and maintained their banks. Every river in China had its own earth-dragon king, who held sway over the waters from a palace far beneath the surface.

Chapter Two

Glittering Gods of the East

In the time of the T'ang Emperors, a thousand years ago, China was a land of wonders, a place where artifice reached heights no Western folk had even dreamed of. The T'ang capital, Ch'ang-an, resting secure behind high, many-gated walls, was laced with tree-lined avenues six hundred feet wide, and the tiled roofs of its palace workshops sheltered craftsmen who could turn rude clay into the most translucent of porcelains, transform dull ore into burnished sculptures that seemed to breathe with their own life, fashion gauzy silks from the cocoons of worms, and shape earth and tree into gardens of jewel-like perfection. Such a garden — ornamented with still lakes placed to mirror the moon and stars, graced with arching bridges and airy viewing pavilions — once served as the lair of two dragons. This garden, described in the elegant calligraphies of the hermit-writer Lu Kuei Meng, belonged to a nobleman who lived in the country not far from Ch'ang-an. He was a collector of natural treasures. Lumbering pandas from the borderlands of Tibet hid shyly among his stands of bamboo; gold-feathered pheasants and laughing thrushes fluttered behind his lat-ticed walls; takins, yaks and Mongolian dromedaries roamed through his wisteria arbors; a Siberian tiger padded through his teahouse; and in the glassy reflecting pool dwelled the dragon pair.

Fed on every delicacy that a mortal could provide, the dragons were domesticated creatures, sluggish from captivity. Day after day, they lay motionless in the sun on an artificial island in the lake, their blue and red scales gleaming, their hooded lids half-closed over yellow eyes. At frequent intervals, they slid into the water and made for the lake's edge, where massive porcelain dishes waited, piled high with cormorant and goose, with roasted swallow and shark, with duck and pig.

Dragons, as Lu Kuei Meng pointed out, were ravenous always: "The great whales in all the seas are not enough to satisfy the appetites of dragons." Perpetually feeding, the captive pair grew soft, and something of their dragon nature seemed to leave them: Earthbound, they bore little resemblance to the wild spirits of wind and water that they once had been.

A day came when a wild dragon soared high above the tiled roofs of the pavilions of the palace. A master of the wind, it rode the air currents on great wings, wheeling and dancing in the patterns of dragon flight. At length, its long-sighted eyes spied the garden, with its silver-leaved willows and its white-blossomed plum trees, and on the glassy lake, it saw two of its own kind, basking in the sun. The dragon descended in easy spirals, until at last it settled on the teahouse roof, bowing the ridgepole with its weight.

It observed the captive dragons; it regarded the bowls piled high with food; and in a voice reverberant with thunder, it spoke in its own speech to them.

"Fly free with me, brothers," it said. "Live in the depths of the waters and soar through the sky. Rest in regions beyond the bounds of air. We are not toys for mortals, but spirits that ride the winds and blow the clouds along."

But the nobleman's dragons were corrupt creatures; indeed, it is possible that their flaccid wings had lost the power of flight. They opened their eyes when the wild creature spoke, but their heavy jaws remained resting on the warmed rock in the lake. The golden eyes slowly closed again. The dragons did not move.

The great voice spoke again: "He who lives with men will die for man." And, unfurling wide-reaching wings to clasp the air, the wild dragon leaped from its perch, soaring in circles higher and higher into the deep blue summer sky, until at last it was lost from view.

Dragons were prescient creatures, and this one's prophecies were fulfilled. Lu Kuei Meng's account does not tell how, but the nobleman's palace was stormed and sacked, its inhabitants put to the sword, its menagerie slaughtered. Only the precious dragons were kept alive, and they were taken in chains to Ch'ang-an, driven in procession down the broad avenues and offered at the palace of the Emperor, as wonders to satisfy the courtiers' idle curiosity. Then the dragons were butchered and eaten.

As the tale of Lu Kuei Meng makes clear, the dragons of Asia differed from those of the West. Like Western dragons, Asian ones were present at the Creation and shared the characteristics of the cosmos—great and primal power, unity with wind and water, links with treasure. Yet Asian dragons—unlike the Western monsters whose rough outline they bore—were creatures of immense complexity, partakers of enchantment. They shared the world with humankind and shared it peaceably, on the whole, despite occasional betrayals on both sides. The Asian dragons had been profoundly linked with mortals from the dawn of history.

The first humans, in fact, were formed by an ancient goddess named Nü Kua who was herself part primal dragon and part mortal. The small creatures she made were tutored by her consort, Fu Hsi, who taught such essential arts as how to weave nets for fishing, how to handle fire, how to make music. They settled into the limited rounds of the mortal world. The dragons descended from Nü Kua, however, were as fluid as the elements. They appeared as frequently in human or animal shape as in dragon form, although they always retained their dragon nature. In China humans regarded these dragons with awe

Queller of the great deluge

The Chinese say that in an ancient age without a beginning or an end, T'ien Ti, the Emperor of Heaven, looked down upon the growing wickedness of the human race and sent a great flood as punishment. Fields of rice were submerged in endless rain, tiled roofs collapsed, and rivers flowed over their banks. Soon much of the earth was covered with water, and the hopes of humanity seemed at an end.

A younger god named Yü took pity on the humans at last, beseeching T'ien Ti to let him save them. T'ien Ti, seeing that the people had indeed suffered enough, relented. He waved his hand, and a gigantic black tortoise plodded forward, bearing on its back magical earth to soak up the floodwaters and form new terrain. Then he summoned an emerald-scaled, winged dragon that joined the young god to help him sculpt the land.

Yü, the tortoise and the dragon descended to the flooded earth. For thirty years they traveled the globe, working so ceaselessly it was said of the god that "the wind was his comb and the rain his bath." They distributed the magical soil, quelling the flood and creating plains here, mountains there. Under Yü's direction, the dragon flew with its tail dipped into the earth; it etched the rivers and scooped out the valleys of a bright new world. Thus was humankind saved from the deluge and destruction.

and with something akin to affection.

The Chinese considered the dragon the primary of four benevolent spiritual animals, the other three being the phoenix, the unicorn and the tortoise. The dragon was unrivaled in wisdom and in its power to confer blessings, and as a result, it came to symbolize that most beneficent of men, the Emperor. (The Emperors of China—linked more closely to their dragon forebears than their subjects—were actually called dragons. Moreover, it was believed that the Emperors possessed dragon blood and that they had dragons in their service. Their affinity with dragons was shown in the imperial accouterments: The Emperor sat on a dragon throne, rode in a dragon boat and slept in a dragon bed. And any representation of the imperial dragon was distinguished from all other dragon effigies or images: Only the Emperor's dragon bore five claws.)

Given the grandeur of the dragon's nature, it is not surprising that in China, long a center for scholarship, a distinguished line of scholars should have devoted such systematic attention to the characters of the dragons that lived among them. They not only defined what a dragon was but also developed schemes for categorizing its age, its position in evolution, its physical attributes, its functions and idiosyncrasies, and the hierarchy that existed within the dragon world.

There was, for instance, the question of dragon birth. It was widely held that the creatures mated in the form of small snakes. The female then deposited eggs near riverbanks, eggs that seemed to be huge stones or jewels. The period of growth in the eggs, as with the dragons themselves, was centuries long. Some people said that a dragon lay thus contained for a thousand years.

The day came, however, when the dragon hatched. Water began to stream from the stones that were the eggs, and the parent dragons let out great cries, one after the other—the first cry to raise the wind, the second to calm it. Then, preceded by cosmic music of thunder, lightning and rain, the shells cracked and the infant creatures wriggled from the shells as small snakes. They began to grow and metamorphose, preparing for their ascent to the sky, which was their true home. Fifteen hundred years were required for a dragon to achieve its full length, five hundred years more to develop their characteristic horns, and one thousand more for the wings to form.

Ultimately, the hatchling became a creature not far different from the Western dragon, but much more closely and carefully observed. The Chinese provided a wealth of detail as to its appearance. For instance, in an article in the *Pan Ts'ao Kang Mu*, the monumental Chinese medical treatise compiled at the end of the 16th Century, the dragon was said to bear "nine resemblances" and to be the largest of scaled creatures. "Its head is like a camel's," the author wrote, "its horns like a deer's, its eyes like a hare's, its ears like a bull's, its neck like a snake's, its belly like a clam's, its scales like a carp's, its claws like an eagle's and its paws like a tiger's. Its scales number eighty-one, being nine by nine;

nine being the extreme lucky number. Its voice is like the beating of a gong. On each side of its mouth are whiskers. Under its throat, the scales are reversed; they jut out twelve inches and can kill a man."

The scholars also made careful categories for dragons. Celestial dragons were said to support the heavens. Spiritual dragons controlled the fall of rain that watered the earth and fed humankind. Earth dragons set the course of rivers, channeling the waters safely to the sea. And subterranean dragons guarded hidden treasure, precious gems, veins of jade and gold. Within each of these categories were four distinct physical types – serpentine, clawed, horned and winged – corresponding, perhaps, to the centuries-long periods of dragon growth.

Other distinctions were found or invented. For instance, dragons were characterized according to their color. Dragons of the purest azure were spectacular omens of dawning spring; their hue was like the eastern sky from whence the rains came at winter's end. Red and black dragons were ferocious beasts, seen sometimes to struggle among the clouds, causing storms that could devastate whole districts at a time. The beast believed to be greater than any of its fellows was colored yellow, like the sun. As elusive as the elements from which it sprang, this enigmatic, august and solitary creature disdained dis-

play. "He can be large or small," wrote one scholar. "Obscure or manifest, short or long, alive or dead: The king cannot drain his pool or catch him. His intelligence and virtue are unfathomable. The yellow dragon does not go in company and does not live in herds. He waits for the wind and the rain and disports himself in the azure air. He wanders in the wilds among the heavens. He comes and goes. At the proper season, if there is perfection, he comes forth; if not, he remains unseen."

Like the yellow dragon, the other creatures of this great race were as uncontrollable as nature itself. The dragon of China was revered and feared first because it manipulated the weather – and the Chinese, like men and women everywhere in those days, lived and died at the will of wind and rain. In fertile southeastern China, along the valleys of the great rivers – the Yellow River, the Yangtze and the Pearl – every hill was terraced with jade green rice paddies, and all through the growing season, the people watched the sky. They needed rain, for rice grew in shallow water, but a storm would make the Yellow River – "China's Sorrow" – overflow its dike-strengthened banks, turning the paddies into a vast, silt-brown inland sea, destroying the crops and leaving the people starving. In the north, too, people watched the

The eggs of China's dragons lay near riverbanks for a thousand years. Their cracking brought furious storms, and as wind and rain raged, small snakes emerged. These grew rapidly into wingless dragons that took to the air by aid of magical crests on their foreheads.

weather with apprehension: The drought and winds that brought storms of sand from the Gobi, covering the towns in a blinding yellow haze and sifting under every door and into every window, meant the fields of wheat and millet that swayed golden in the northern plains would wither; the sheep and goats that speckled the high mountain pastures would die; and again, the people would starve.

The dragon was the Rain Master. Its eyes flashed lightning, its flight was the wind; its very breath condensed to form the rain—not only the gentle rains of spring and summer that wreathed the mountain peaks in clouds of mist, but the fierce storms that bent the crops and flooded the valleys.

It was said that in winter—the dry season—the dragons were hibernating in the depths of the rivers and lakes, at rest in water, their native element. Only later, in spring, did they ascend into the sky, and only then did the winds begin to blow—the warm west winds, the gales from the north and the whirlwinds and waterspouts

formed by the dragons' spiral paths to the skies. After that came the rains—unless in their soaring the dragons flew too high into the heavens, leaving the earth small and dry beneath them.

So the people prayed to dragons. Each river, every lake and even the small pools of China sheltered dragon kings who were the waters' guardians, and at the edges of the waters, if the rains were late, the farmers banged gongs and cymbals, seeking to awaken the sleeping spirits. The people made offerings of small images, fashioned roughly from clay. Sometimes these rituals were successful and sometimes not, for the dragon in its underwater realm was remote and clothed in mystery.

As the peasants worked in long, single lines stretched across the paddies—their bodies bent almost double, their hands deep in the cool mud, where they buried the seedling rice plants one by one—they told what they knew of the dragon world hidden beneath the waters of China. The little boys who led the dappled water buffaloes heard the tales, as did the tiny chil-

dren strapped to their mothers' backs, and so the stories were preserved, passed down through the years from parent to child.

The people spoke of splendors as they sweated in the sun. Within the cool depths of the rivers, they said, were palaces made of a stone so lucid that all the life of the river — the darting fish, the nets of the fishermen and the keels of their boats above — could be seen by those who lived within the walls. The columns of the palaces were formed from jade and adorned with silver filigree; the doors were carved of creamy ivory; and the thrones were made of rosy coral branches, glowing with gold and ornamented with pearls.

And in the shimmering light of those underwater kingdoms, the shapes of the dragon folk danced and shifted, so that now they appeared in true dragon form — horned and crested, clawed and scaled — and now as the most beautiful of mortals, brighter and braver than any earthly prince, with ancient eyes that were wise and gay.

Or so said the laborers in the fields, who passed their lives with never a sight of the dragon race, other than clouds and mist and the slanting rains that provided sustenance. Converse with dragons was a matter for Emperors and adventurers, not for poor men tied to the soil. And traffic with those unpredictable beings, the poor peasants thought, might easily lead to strange transformations, as the tale of Liu Ye showed:

Liu Ye was a young scholar who lived during the reign of the T'ang Emperor Kao-tsung, and his adventure began on the day he left the broad avenues and rich palaces of Ch'ang-an to return to his humble home in Shensi Province. He had failed the annual examination that decided which scholars were admitted to the elite corps of imperial administrators, and his spirits were low.

He set a good pace, however, walking on narrow lanes through the orchards of peach trees and along the richly terraced slopes that lay near the Imperial City. Ch'ang-an's gates were some hours behind him when he reached the banks of the Ching River. He paused among the willows to rest in the heat of the afternoon.

Sharleen Collicott

The air was very still; no other travelers passed along that dusty road, and Liu Ye sat alone, staring at the water. Presently he heard the dull clapping of bells and saw a flock of goats tripping briskly along the path. They clustered around him curiously, examining him through their dark, oblong pupils; but when the goatherd called, they scattered among the trees, browsing on the leaves.

The goatherd was a woman dressed in rags, but she was clearly no rough peasant. The hair that lay around her shoulders shone as glossy as a raven's wing; her skin had the faint glow of peach blossoms, and her hands were as soft as an infant's, not roughened with labor, as a peasant woman's would be. Her eyes were the perfect almond shape of a court lady's, but here was a curious thing: They were not brown or black, but as green as the river waters. Liu Ye greeted her courteously, and she sat down beside him and told him her tale.

She was a Princess of the dragon race, the daughter of the Dragon King of Lake Tungt'ing, 400 miles to the southeast, and she had been given in marriage to the Prince of this river. But the Ching Dragon Prince, to her bewilderment, had neither loved her nor accorded her the honor due his wife: He had placed her under an enchantment and cast her out to walk in mortal form upon the dry land as a goat girl. Exiled from the watery realm of her own kind, she could not even speak to seek the help of her dragon father.

Liu Ye was a compassionate man, and her story moved him: He offered to help her if he could. She told him how she might be freed. He must go, she said, to the distant lake that was her home. Beside the lake he would find a tall pine tree. If Liu Ye struck the tree three times with his sash, he would summon from the dragon kingdom a herald, who would conduct him safely to her father's palace; and if he then told her father of her plight, help would surely come.

Thus Liu Ye, who was brave as well as compassionate, found himself making the long and lonely journey to the mountain lake of Tungt'ing. It took him a month, but at last he stood beside the calm waters, watching the reflections of the clouds slide across their surface. He found the aged pine at the verge of the water, and

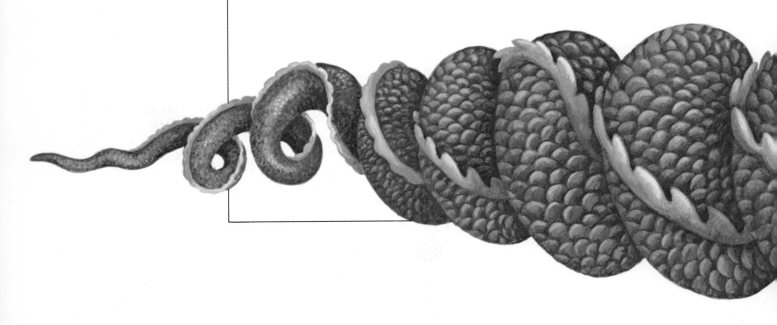

Some scholars held that dragons developed from mere water snakes, which, after five centuries of growth, assumed the primary dragon form—a serpent with a carp's head.

with his sash, he struck it three times.

At the final blow, the waters near the shore bubbled and tumbled, and from them emerged a tall young man, clad in the armor of a royal guard and bearing a broad-bladed, gold-hilted sword.

The warrior raised his sword in salute. Liu Ye told his tale and asked, with some diffidence, to be taken to the court of the Dragon King.

The bright sword described a glittering arc in the air; then the light faded before Liu Ye's eyes, and he slept. He knew not how long he remained so, but he awoke to a wondrous sight.

He stood in a great hall, bathed in nacreous light, between two rows of motionless courtiers whose silken robes stretched to the floor in unmoving, sculptured folds and whose branching headdresses were hung with chains of gold. Far ahead of him, at the end of the corridor formed by the courtiers, a dais crowned by a throne of lapis lazuli, rose in a halo of light. On the throne, with his long hands clasped loosely on the jade tablet that signified his rank, sat the Dragon King in his mortal form.

"Advance, mortal," said a low voice near the young man's ear, and Liu Ye moved forward between the shining ranks of courtiers until he stood before the King. The young man bowed.

"Speak," said the King. Then Liu Ye told of the plight of the Dragon Princess. As a token of his truth, he offered the King a small tablet, inscribed with characters in the Princess' fine hand.

The King took the tablet and examined it. Finally he rose, his face like stone. Sounds stirred among the people of his court—first whispering, then weeping and then the high, formal wailing that signified grief. Instantly, the King raised his hand, palm out, and spoke.

"Silence," he said. "Do not arouse the vessel of wrath."

The Dragon King spoke too late, it seemed. The glassy walls of the hall swayed as if in a winter wind, and the waters outside whirled and foamed. Through the palace corridors echoed a ululating scream. Liu Ye heard a crackle and roar of flame. Then the vermilion streak of a dragon rushed past the archway that led to the

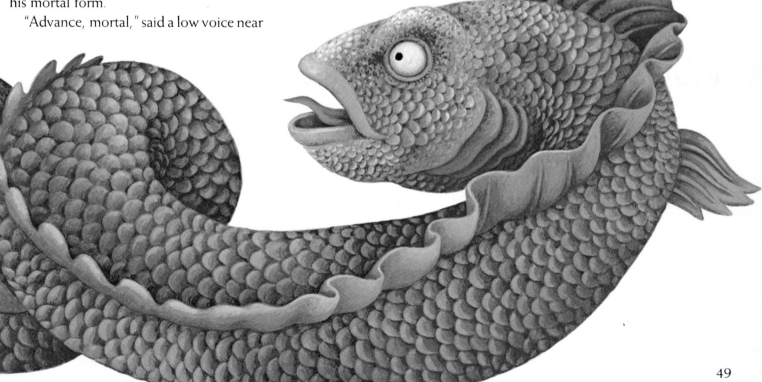

hall, spurting fire and dragging — by chains lashed around its enormous legs — the shattered remains of a great column. The scaled sides seemed to flash by for hours, but eventually the archway was empty again and the demented screaming faded into the distance. A profound silence settled onto the court.

White-faced, Liu Ye turned to the throne. The Dragon King shrugged massively. He sat upon the throne, placed his hands upon his knees and told the mortal something of the world of dragons.

The mighty dragon was Chien Tang, the King's own brother, chained in the depths of the palace because of his savagery: Chien Tang's boiling, seething, elemental rages were untempered by the wisdom that controlled most dragons' power, and destruction trailed him always: He

was a bringer of catastrophe, of storm and fire and flood, and therefore had been condemned to perpetual imprisonment by the Emperor of Heaven, the god who ruled all dragons. Devoid of any shade of humaneness, Chien Tang lacked the freedom to assume mortal form; he wore his beast shape always. Now, fired by the love of kin, he had broken from his bonds, and his vengeful nature took free rein. He had gone to rescue his brother's daughter.

Long moments passed. The Dragon King sat upon his lapis throne; the courtiers waited in silence; and the mortal waited with them.

Then once again the Dragon King rose. He beckoned to a figure who had appeared at the archway of the hall. In silence, the figure advanced to the throne. It was a man — almost as tall as the Dragon King

The serpentine dragon required a millennium of growth to achieve a more dragon-like appearance — four clawed feet and an elongated face, surrounded by a shaggy beard and a flying mane of hair. This was its second form of being.

himself—and in the sheltering curve of his silk-clad arm, still dressed in the rags of a goatherd, stood the Dragon Princess. She saw Liu Ye and ducked her head shyly, but before her face was hidden, the mortal glimpsed her sweet smile.

The Dragon King drew his daughter into his arms and spoke over her head to the man who had brought her safely home.

"Well, Brother," the King said. "It seems you have been given freedom."

Then Chien Tang bowed and told his story. Charged with his dragon fury, trailing winds and lashing rains, he had flown to the Ching River and torn its waters from their bed. He had found the palace of the Ching Dragon Prince and killed the Prince. In a single breath, Chien Tang had reduced the proud palace to shining shards.

But in rescuing and avenging the Princess, he had learned something. His love for her had given him eyes to see the cost of violence: The rains and floods brought about by his wrath had drowned the crops and buried hundreds of peasant houses up to their eaves. Thousands of Chinese farmers were dead, lying tangled in the mud of the Ching River. Chien Tang, therefore, had flown to the roof of the sky, to the Emperor of Heaven himself. Before the celestial throne, he wept for the ravages of his rage and told its cause. And thus, having learned the pain of mortal sorrows, Chien Tang was granted the choice of mortal form and freed

from the punishment that had been laid upon him years before.

When Chien Tang had finished speaking, curious things began to happen in the crystal hall. The King himself stood calmly by his throne, his daughter beside him and the mortal Liu Ye beside his daughter. But all around them, the sudden chattering of the courtiers rose like the twittering and trilling of thousands of birds, like the liquid songs of flutes or the chiming of bells. In the pearly light, the courtiers' shapes seemed to dissolve and form again and again, as if the very atoms of creation were dancing. Where men and women had stood, Liu Ye saw the flashing of birds' wings, the sparkling coils of dragons' bodies and the gleam of dragons' eyes; he saw skipping fawns and prancing horses, dancing leopards, and serpents that spouted flame. A ringing voice sounded in Liu Ye's

Sharleen Collicott

ear. "Be one with us, mortal," the Dragon King said. And he placed his daughter's hand in that of Liu Ye and smiled.

Thus, in an instant, Liu Ye lost his earthbound nature and became one of the race that lived in the air and in water as well. He felt the silver cold of lake water and saw a thick mist of cloud – but he was himself water and cloud, roiling and shapeless. An image of dragons came to him, and his vision cleared. He was under a blue sky, resting on a wind that stretched and pulled his powerful wings wide, warmed by a sun that beat upon his curving back. Below him were towering white mountains of mist, and beside him was a creature made in his own image, crested and shining, with great emerald eyes. It was the Dragon King's daughter. She soared with Liu Ye on the wind, swooping and leaping, matching him turn for turn and dive for dive. Then, the pair banked and plunged together through the cool cloud layer. Wheeling, they headed for the waters of Lake Tungt'ing.

As they winged homeward, their dragon eyes scanned the tiny landscape beneath them and spied the mountains with their terraces of rice, the winding rivers and toy villages. In the distance they saw, as strictly fashioned as a chessboard, the streets, red-roofed pavilions and walls that marked the Imperial City, Ch'ang-an, where the scholar Liu Ye would never go again. The dragons laughed a wild laugh and sped swiftly on, and far below them, the small mortals heard the peal of distant thunder.

As the story of Liu Ye the scholar

The dragon reached full maturity after three thousand years, when it acquired branchlike arcs of wings that carried it through the highest reaches of the heavens.

shows, a mortal – if his deeds were brave and his heart great – could hope to ascend to the realm of dragons and dance upon the wind with them. Even humbler creatures could aspire to the dragon state, or so the storytellers said.

In Honan Province each spring, for instance, migrating carp in their thousands swam up the rushing Yellow River to challenge a particularly rough stretch of rapids called the Dragon Gate. Those few who leaped past the foaming, singing waterfall – only seventy-one succeeded each year, it was said – were greeted by a maelstrom of rain, wind and fire. Entering this primal turbulence as fish, they emerged as noble dragons. People made from the tale an analogy for their own lives: Scholars who passed the daunting annual civil service examinations – the more successful brethren of Liu Ye – were said to "leap through the Dragon Gate."

Such analogies were common in every walk of Chinese life. Like the warriors of the West, with their dragon banners and dragon shields, the Chinese sought to endow themselves with something of the dragons' nature by making images of the mighty beasts. The Asian dragons, however, served many causes besides valor.

Nine different dragons, whose traits or passions made them appropriate to the subjects they adorned, protected mortal objects. Thus, P'u lao, a dragon famous for crying loudly when attacked, was carved on bells and gongs. Ch'iu-niu, a

Shaking the foundations of the palace of a Dragon King, a thousand-foot-long
serpent bent on vengeance burst the chains that bound him and flew to freedom.

spirit of music, was pictured on the zither—ch'in. Pi hsi, lover of the word, was etched on stone tablets used for writing. Strong Pa hsia held up the foot of heavy monuments. The valiant Chao fêng protected the steep eaves of temples. The water dragon Ch'ih wên appeared on bridges and—as a fire prevention—rooftops. Suan ni was a quiet, watchful beast, depicted on the throne of the meditative Buddha. The truculent Yai tzŭ was inscribed on swords. And the last, Pi han, was a quarrelsome creature seen on the gates of prisons. Even more powerful than images were the physical parts of dragons. Some beasts, it seemed, returned to the earth when they died, and their bodies, bereft of cloud and fire, could still provide wonders. Certain parts of the body, for instance, made cures for the ills of humanity: The medical encyclopedias of ancient China were full of prescriptions. The bones—in particular, the spine, when ground to powder—could be used to cure gallstones, infantile fevers, paralysis of the legs and the ailments of pregnant women. The teeth were efficacious in the treatment of madness and headache. The brain and liver were prized specifics against dysentery. Nor were the virtues of dragons' bodies solely medicinal. Dragon skin was said

to glow in the dark, and the fat burned so brilliantly that the flames were visible hundreds of miles away. Dragon blood turned to precious amber when it touched the ground, the sages said. And the spittle of the great creatures formed the basis of the rarest perfumes and the most permanent dyes. It was said that an Emperor of the Sung Dynasty used the spittle of a purple dragon to make an ink with which he inscribed the names of his most honored ministers and sages on tablets of jade, gold and crystal. To obtain an adequate supply of the ink, he had a dragon reared in his palace compound. It salivated when it was offered roasted swallows, a particularly cherished food of dragons.

There also was a dragon part of almost-mythic power, seen by few and coveted by all. This was the dragon's pearl. Said to be possessed by dragons who guarded precious treasure, the pearl was a jewel of extraordinary size and luminosity, usually carried in the side pockets of the dragon's jaw, or in folds beneath the chin. The pearls emitted their own wondrous light, which never dimmed and had the power to illuminate a house of many pavilions. It also was a vessel of power and health, and anything it touched grew and multiplied. It had an even greater power for mortals, as a tale from Szechwan Province shows.

On a small, poor farm in the southern part of the province lived a young boy and his widowed mother, who eked out a meager existence by toiling in the rice paddies of their more prosperous neighbors and by tending a small vegetable garden. The boy went to the river to draw water each day, carrying his yoke fitted with two wooden

To propitiate the dragons that were masters of the winds and rains, the Chinese made offerings of lotus flowers and food.

water buckets. As he returned along the dusty road, he passed a meadow, and here he often stopped to cut grass as fodder for his single goat. After resting a while on the turf, he would gather up the grass, shoulder the yoke again and head for home.

Eventually he noticed a curious thing: No matter how hot and dry the sun in summer or how fierce and cold the winter rains, the meadow stayed lush and green.

It seemed forever caught at the very height of spring. The boy pondered about this for several days, and finally he took a spade to the meadow and dug a square of grass-covered sod, thinking to plant it in his garden so that his vegetables, like the meadow, would thrive.

As he lifted the square of cut sod, however, a luminous white sphere rolled from it to the ground and lay there gleaming.

Reclaiming an Emperor's gift

In Japan, they told this story of a dragon's power and a maiden's love and courage:

It happened once that a sacred pearl was sent by sea from China to the Japanese court. It was lost on the voyage, however, to the dragon that ruled that part of the ocean. The tale is unclear about how this happened; in any event, the official responsible for the jewel, Lord Kamatari, was sent into exile for the loss.

Kamatari retired to the small fishing village of Fukazaki, near the Sea of Japan. He lived quietly among the villagers for some months, and eventually he fell in love with one of them – an *ama*, a woman who made her living by diving for shellfish.

He loved the woman dearly, but even her presence did not cure him of his grief at his failure and exile. When he told her his story, however, she determined to prove her love for him.

She bade Kamatari sail with her to a place on the sea far from shore. Once there, she plunged from the boat into the depths of the ocean, holding her breath as she skimmed jagged coral reefs and tunneled through the thick seaweed that hid the dragon's palace. She gained the palace quickly, and inside she found the precious pearl.

The *ama* snatched the prize and fled, thrusting through the waters toward the boat and Kamatari. But she had been seen. The raging myrmidons of the Dragon King – octopus, fish, tortoises, crabs and even a wild-haired *oni*, or devil – were moving swiftly through the waves toward her, intent on retrieving the jewel.

In desperation, she slit open her breast with her knife and pressed the pearl into the flesh to keep it from harm. Then, with both hands free, she made for the boat.

She reached it at last. The monsters fell back, and Kamatari pulled the *ama* to safety. She gave him his jewel as proof of her love, but the wound she had made was fatal, and in a few moments, the woman died.

The boy saw how it glowed, and his eyes widened at its beauty. He picked it up. It was warm in his hand.

Knowing that such a jewel was of great value, he took it home and hid it away. For safety, he placed it in the nearly empty pottery jar that held the household's rice. Then he planted the sod in the garden.

Early the next morning, the boy went out to pick vegetables for his mother while the dew was still on them. The grass he had planted the night before had withered and died. He stared at it in some surprise, and while he gazed, he heard a shrill cry from within the house.

The boy ran into the hut at once, and there he found his mother pointing at the corner where the rice jar stood. It had filled to the brim during the night. The boy knelt and plunged his hand deep into the

59

rice, spilling mounded grains. He drew out the pearl, and its light glowed pink through the flesh of his hand. The dark little room took on a rosy glow. His mother gasped, for she knew what she saw. It was a dragon's pearl the boy had found. Neither mother nor son had any idea of how it had come to be in the meadow, but it did not matter: The pearl meant their good health and good fortune. The woman showed her son its powers. She took the pearl from him and placed it gently in the jar of oil that stood beside the rice jar, and as the pair watched, the oil rose slowly until it filled the jar.

In the days that followed, mother and son made the garden thrive, the goat flow with milk, the chickens double their laying and the ducks grow fat. They kept the pearl, their precious treasure, carefully concealed, but it was impossible to hide the results of its presence. Whispers began in the village — first curious, then envious. Their neighbors, it was clear, were growing hostile. At length, the headman of the village took it upon himself to discover the cause of the family's new prosperity.

One morning, unannounced, he stepped through the door of the house, ducking to avoid the low lintel. He found a glowing room crowded with jars of rice, wheat and millet. Piled in a basket were gleaming silks. Glittering on the floor was a pile of coins, and the boy and his mother were crouched beside them, counting quickly and chuckling as they did so. In one hand, the boy clutched the lustrous pearl.

Quick as a flash, the headman seized the child, but the boy popped the pearl into his mouth. Cheek bulging, he stared defiantly up at the headman, who lifted the child by his shoulders and began to shake him. The result was dreadful: With a cough, the boy swallowed the pearl.

Curious villagers had clustered outside the house by now. They were astonished to see the headman backing out the door, pale and shaking. Before he could speak he was pushed aside by a huge man with flashing eyes and wildly floating hair. The man growled unintelligible words and, pushing through the villagers, made off in a leaping run for the river. At its bank, he dropped to his knees, furiously gulping water and groaning ceaselessly to himself. Wisps of smoke curled from his nostrils; tongues of flame licked at his hair.

Then the world itself seemed to alter. Lightning cracked and thunder rumbled. Rain clouds swallowed the morning light. The huge man writhed to the drumbeats of the storm. His head grew even more massive, and his body sank to the ground. On his back perched a shadow, a cloudy, shapeless mass. Lightning flashed again, bathing the riverbank and the trees in a white glare. In that instant, the villagers saw a dragon stretching powerful wings to leap into the air. It wheeled above them and, with a scream, dived into the river. Where it entered the water, a column of steam rose. The pearl had found a rightful home again; a new dragon had been made.

The tale did not tell what happened to the boy's mother. She might have been honored or pitied by the other villagers; she might have been scorned or, after a while, ignored. But the last is unlikely, for the woman was the mother of a son who had ascended to become part of the forces of nature, at one with the cosmos.

And that exalted state was the heart of the dragon race of Asia. It is true that the dragons of China and Japan could assume the characters of beasts or humans, and could be kept as captives or as pets. Their habits in those manifestations were discussed in the most trivial terms, as if dragons were no more than the tiny, silky dogs that court ladies carried in their sleeves. Chinese dragons, for instance, were said to fear a baffling set of objects: iron, beeswax, centipedes, tigers, and even silk thread dyed in five colors.

Yet the great dragons—those that existed in a state far beyond the mortals' ken—were more than beasts and more than men. They were regarded with curiosity and affection, it is true, but also with awe. Prayers were said to them and offerings made to obtain their favor, for these dragons flew among the stars and clouds and conversed with the gods. Indeed, people saw them as godlike creatures. Masters of the elements and riders of the wind, they appeared to mortals appareled in celestial light and trailing clouds of glory.

Amid the furies of gales at sea, China's sailors sometimes saw the storm bringers—dragons that leaped among the waves and through the ocean mist and roiled the waters in their sport.

A MAID WHO BRAVED THE DEEP

In Japan, where dragons crueler than those of China ruled the elements, a tale celebrated a woman's valor in an encounter with one such beast.

Long ago, an Emperor banished a famous warrior to the Oki Islands, in the storm-wracked Sea of Japan. The reason for the punishment is not known. The offense may well have been a minor one, for the Emperor suffered greatly from an illness that had come upon him suddenly, and his temper was uncertain. In any case, the samurai was taken under guard to the place of exile. He left behind a daughter, Tokoyo, who was as pretty as a chrysanthemum and as strong as the steel of her father's sword.

She mourned, but she was a brave young woman, and soon she set out to find her father. For weeks Tokoyo traveled alone along the coast of the great island of Honshu, until she came to Hoki Province in the north. From the rocks there

she could see, faint in the sea mist, the silhouette of the isle where her father was imprisoned. But she could find no sailor or fisherman to take her across the water, because it was well known that the Oki Islands were haunted by dragons.

Night fell, and in the concealing darkness, Tokoyo stole a small fishing boat. She rowed the little craft through the waves for hours. The moon set, the sun rose, and still she rowed. Not until late the next day did she reach her destination. Leaving the boat on the rocky shore, Tokoyo followed a path to a road cut into the coastal cliffs. She came to a shrine, and there she lay down and slept.

On the following morning, faint sounds of weeping awakened her. At once she scrambled to her feet and followed the road to its end on a windy headland, where she discovered a piteous scene.

At the edge of the cliff, high above the seething sea, stood a maiden robed in white, and near her knelt two aged people — her parents. They were sobbing uncontrollably. Behind them

stood a priest, his head bowed.

It was a sacrifice, the priest explained. Each year the people of that island gave a maiden to the dragon Yofuné-Nushi, ruler of the deep and bringer of storms, and the offering held off the tempests the creature could send.

Impulsively, Tokoyo offered to take the maiden's place. She put on the ceremonial white kimono, clasped a warrior's dagger between her teeth and, without hesitation, leaped into the boiling waves.

Down through the green depths she plummeted, swimming as strongly as she had in her childhood, when she dived with the pearl fishers of her own province. She neared the sea bottom, and there she found a cave mouth. Beside it was a curiosity – a wooden statue of the Emperor who had banished her father. And streaming from the opening was an undulating serpent with dagger-like claws and luminous scales.

It glided swiftly toward her, eyes alight with fury and anticipation, and Tokoyo struck at it. She thrust her dagger in-

to one of the creature's eyes; half-blinded, the dragon lashed at her clumsily. The woman struck again. Then the end came quickly: The dragon sank to the ocean floor, its coils slowly stirred by the tide.

Charged with a greater-than-mortal strength, the dragon-slayer grasped the serpent with one hand and the statue with the other and kicked her way back to the surface.

When the priest and the others saw her head appear above the waves, they ran down to the shore and stretched out helping hands.

The ending of the tale was wonderful and strange. Tokoyo was taken with her prizes to the lord of that island, who greatly honored her bravery. He sent messengers to the Emperor about her feat and thus discovered the meaning of the statue. When the image, which had been cursed and thrown to the sea-god, was removed from the water, the Emperor's illness disappeared. In his gratitude, the ruler reunited the woman and her father and brought them back to their homeland.

Chapter Three

The Serpent Ascendant

Long before the scourge of conquest oppressed the people of Britain – before the Romans arrived, shivering in the unfamiliar cold, to linger four centuries until the unruly Saxons stormed across the North Sea and replaced them as masters – the island was racked by another, stranger misfortune. It happened each year on the Eve of Beltane – or May Day Eve – the time, ironically enough, for festivals celebrating the reawakening of the earth. On that evening, however, high above the cloud tops, two dragons battled in the air. One was red, one white. Locked in a monstrous embrace, snarling and steaming, clawing and tearing, they writhed across the heavens like some vast and fiery wheel, until the white dragon pushed the red far beyond the fringes of the island.

None of this was observed by the people in the land below. But on that eve each year, as the last light of day faded, the red dragon's battle howl swelled in the stillness. It echoed across the western downs and the northern heaths, rang from the gray crags of Wales and burst over the little settlement of London. And everywhere the shriek was heard, it left a wake of terror. It was no more than noise – a noise that increased to a hateful, deafening volume and slowly died. But the sound had a ghoulish power. Although villagers and townsfolk alike took shelter behind barred doors and shuttered windows on that night, the terrible sound rattled the walls, pouring in through every crack and cranny like the icy breath of the winter wind. When they heard it, men and women blanched and trembled; the children whimpered and buried their faces in their mothers' skirts.

The fearsome noise brought blight. Pregnant women miscarried when they heard it, and for days afterward, cows gave no milk and hens would not lay. Some said that even growth in the newly sowed fields paused for a week or so after the dreadful echo had died away. The luxuriance of summer eventually blunted the memory of the blight, but with each passing year the vigor of the land and people ebbed.

Generation after generation was thus afflicted until a King named Lludd ascended to the throne. He was a good King, just and wise, and brought a measure of prosperity to Britain. Yet each year, with the first blush of spring, the air was shattered with savage screaming, and the people continued to weaken. The King sought the advice of his brother Llevelys, a ruler in France who was adept at magic.

Legend has it that in those times evil spirits traveled invisible in the air, spying on mortals and foiling their attempts at order. The two Kings therefore met at sea. A curious protocol surrounded their conference. They sat together in a small boat, rocking at anchor in the gray waters off the French coast, and they spoke through a horn of brass that held their words secure. Evil ears could catch the faintest whisper on the wind, it was said.

Llevelys had the answer. He told his brother of the battle of the dragons that caused the screaming, and he told Lludd how to end it.

"Here is what you must do," Llevelys whispered into the tube of brass. "Send out scholars and mapmakers; have them compass the kingdom to find its exact center. On the Eve of Beltane next, dig a pit waist-deep there, and in it set a caldron of mead, covered with a silken cloth. Drag a stone chest to the very edge of the pit.

"In the sky above the meadow a tumult will sound, and fleeting shapes will appear, black against the clouds. First will be seen a pair of taloned eagles, tearing at each other. They will change into bears, cuffing and bellowing, and then into fighting cocks, showering feathers and blood. Last of all, you will see the red and white dragons in their true shapes for an instant before they drop as piglets from the sky. Still scrapping and squealing, the piglets will plunge into the caldron, taking the silken cloth with them. They will drink their fill of mead and sleep.

"When they are quite still, bind them up in the cloth, lift them from the caldron and seal them in the chest. Then carry it to some remote, cliff-bound corner of Britain and bury it deep in the living rock. Thus imprisoned, the dragons will trouble your realm no longer."

All happened as Llevelys had foretold. The center of the country was found to lie in a meadow near Oxford—a finding that later geographers would dispute. There, through the magic of the pit, the mead and the silken cloth, the dragons were captured and closed in a great stone chest. The chest was buried in the barren expanse of Dinas Emrys, a shelflike projection on the flank of Snowdon, the highest mountain in Wales. Every May Day Eve from that year forth passed in peace and silence.

But other ills—invasion and servitude—tried the souls of Britons over the centuries that followed. And it was war that drove men back to the heights of Dinas Emrys, five hundred years after the dragons were interred there, and long after memory of them had faded. The Romans had come and gone, and their successors as conquerors, the Saxons, seemed sure of victory. An embattled King of the Britons named Vortigern sought to build a stronghold to defend his diminished realm. He chose the flat-topped expanse of Dinas Emrys. But construction of the fortress made no headway. The site of the great stronghold was as level as a tabletop, and the walls were made of mountain granite, cunningly joined, yet they would not hold. Every afternoon, the walls erected that morning began to shift and skew, and overnight they tumbled into ruins.

The wizard Merlin, at that time still a boy, unknotted the mystery. Beneath the building site, he declared, lay a pit, flooded by centuries of rain. The boggy, unsteady ground covering the pit doomed construction to failure, but there was more to be revealed, for in the depths of the underground pool lay a great stone chest, and in that chest were imprisoned two dragons, sleeping as they had slept for five hundred years.

At a word from the King, the workers began to excavate. Water oozed wherever their spades bit the earth, and soon the soil crumbled beneath their feet and clods floated away in an upwelling pool of peat-colored water. A channel was dug to the edge of the plateau to drain the pit, and an ancient chest was levered from the muck.

A boy knelt beside it to chisel open the hasp. Then a ripple of fear swept over the watching crowd as the lid flew back and a billow of smoke rose from the interior, followed by a lick of flame. Two dark shapes loomed within the smoke, swelling like genies from a bottle, until they towered over the treeless mountainside. Scales glittered through the smoky veil, and the crowd scattered as it discerned a pair of dragons. Bat wings beating thunderously, flames jetting from their maws, tails corkscrewing, they struggled up into clear air.

There the two dragons, one dirty white and the other mottled red, resumed their age-old struggle, grappling and flaring and slashing, white dragon in pursuit of red, red dragon in pursuit of white, until the sky was crisscrossed with smoke trails, the turf was scorched, and Vortigern and his courtiers gasped in the sulfurous pall. At last the white dragon tired, and the red dragon saw within its grasp the victory that had eluded it for so long. Exultantly, it chased the white dragon toward the lofty crown of Snowdon. No bigger than a sparrow, the white dragon disappeared over the crag, but the red dragon paused at the summit, rampant in triumph, a dark silhouette tipped with bright flame. Then it too vanished, and the dragons were never again seen—or heard—in Britain.

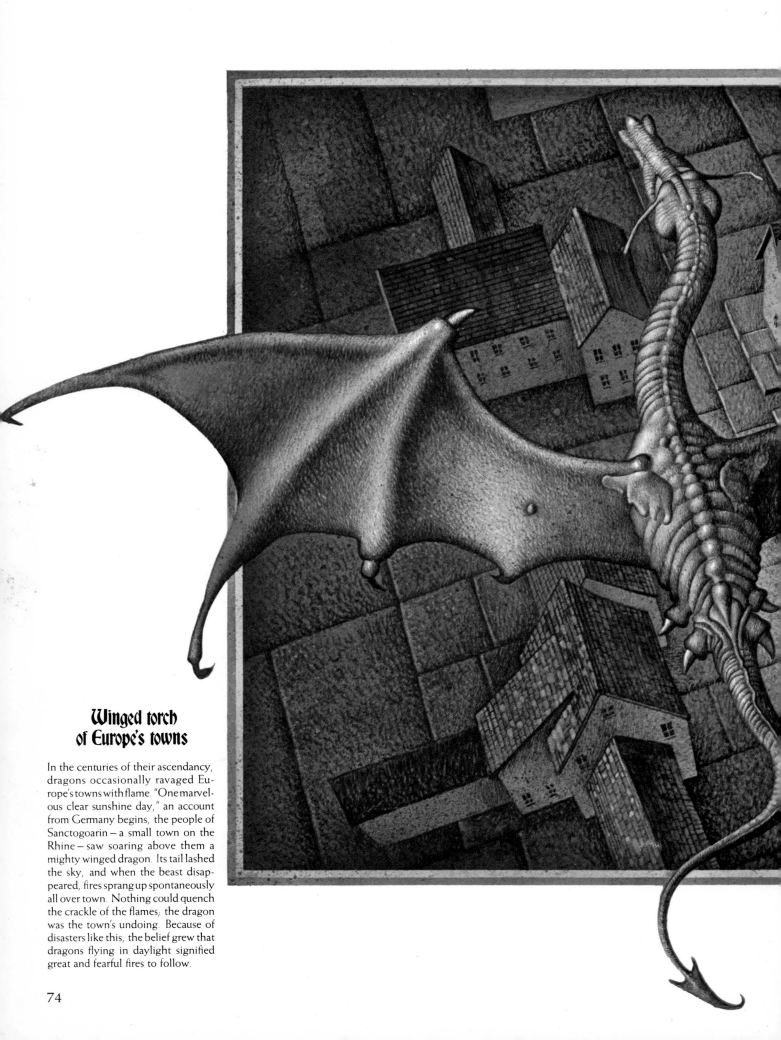

Winged torch of Europe's towns

In the centuries of their ascendancy, dragons occasionally ravaged Europe's towns with flame. "One marvelous clear sunshine day," an account from Germany begins, the people of Sanctogoarin – a small town on the Rhine – saw soaring above them a mighty winged dragon. Its tail lashed the sky, and when the beast disappeared, fires sprang up spontaneously all over town. Nothing could quench the crackle of the flames; the dragon was the town's undoing. Because of disasters like this, the belief grew that dragons flying in daylight signified great and fearful fires to follow.

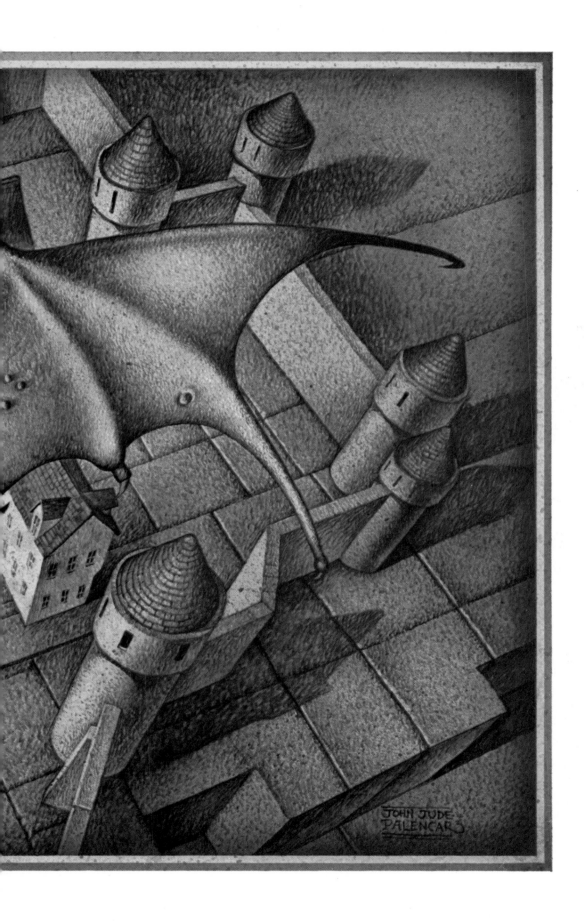

Few accounts of the dragons that beleaguered Europe have so grand a sweep. It was rare that a dragon was chronicled over a span of five hundred years, rarer still that a single dragon blighted an entire land. But in other respects the tale is unexceptional. The evil spread by the dragon's cry mirrored on a large scale the sufferings of towns and hamlets all across Europe in the days of the dragons' ascendancy.

It was not always easy to distinguish the ravages of a dragon from disasters that had other roots. A flood might follow a heavy rainstorm, but a river might also surge over its banks when, far upstream, a dragon roiled the waters with its tail. Famine often resulted from caprices of weather; but a nearby dragon, with a limitless appetite for livestock, and breath that scorched or poisoned fields, also could starve the populace. When the waters of a village well grew bitter and emetic, the cause lay less often in the workings of rock and rain than in a poisonous dragon, lurking in the well itself or in a nearby mine.

Thus dragons' activities threatened the very underpinnings of human existence. And dragons were not occasional intruders or distant menaces, but permanent tenants of the same world as that inhabited by humanity. Unlike their ancestors—the cosmic dragons that girdled the earth's midriff, gnawed at the frame of creation or raged at the rising of the sun—these latter-day dragons were very much creatures of nature. They bulked in caves and chasms; they coiled around hills and ancient grave tumuli; they trailed stench and slime through forests; they mingled with the shadows in springs and rivers.

How they came to populate the face of Europe is an enigma. Some, the direct descendants of primal chaos, seemed to have haunted their shadowy niches since time immemorial; others were known to have hatched from leathery eggs; still others, haunters of grave mounds, coalesced from the fetid vapors of the tomb.

Whatever their origins, the dragons that beset Europe were the agents of age-old disorder. They were the enemies of settlement and cultivation, and a barrier to civilization's conquest of the great wilderness that cloaked Europe.

It is no surprise that many venerable towns of Europe still preserve the memory of a local dragon in their names, for the defeat of that dragon was the act that solidly grounded the settlement, enabling it to persist and flourish. A multitude of English hamlets have names beginning with *worm* or *orme*—Worms Head, Great Ormes Head, Ormesleigh, Ormeskirk, Wormelow and Wormeslea, for instance—and in every case the names commemorate the dragons, known in the English countryside as worms, that were slain early in the history of the districts. In Wales, a village called Denbigh echoes in its name the cry of the hero who defeated a dragon there, making the region safe for human settlement: *"Dim bych!"* meaning "Thou mayest not be!"

No single victory was decisive, however. The advance of humanity into the wilderness was fitful, and setbacks were all too frequent. In those perilous days, catastrophe could strike even the most set-

The coming of a dragon could be silent and secret: In England once, a youth tossed a worm into a village well. The creature grew in the darkness until it became a monster—which proceeded to terrorize the district of Lambton for seven long years.

tled and orderly parts of humankind's domain, for the forces of nature, although held at bay with ceaseless toil, were by no means conquered. Plagues, droughts and cruel winters took their toll, and the beasts of the forest sometimes slouched into Europe's largest cities. But the most shocking instance of the capricious and ungovernable powers threatening to undo the careful work of civilization was the appearance, in districts long ago cleared and put to the plow, of a dragon.

Some dragons burst over the horizon with fire and commotion, their threat apparent from the first. But others arrived with an insidious lack of drama, as treacherous and unpredictable as the physical world they lived in. Such was the case at the castle of Lambton, on the River Wear in the north of England.

It was Childe Lambton, the heir to the castle, who first beheld the dragon. Young and careless then, he guessed nothing of the peril it presented. One Sunday, while his father and his neighbors were at Mass, the youth stood on the bank of the Wear, fishing for salmon. He cast his line into the icy current again and again, but not a fish did he catch. Hours passed. At length he began irritably to curse the river.

Then the young lord felt a powerful jolt. Bit by bit, he brought his line in, needing all of his strength. At last he saw what he had caught. A glistening black worm, no longer than a thumb, thrashed and danced on his hook.

The youth caught the creature in one hand and held it up to inspect it. It writhed with startling power, the narrow body flexing and slipping between his fingers. It had the broad head and wide mouth of a salamander, but its fangs were those of a viper, delicate and needle-sharp. It was slimed with a milky ooze, and its sides were pitted with a row of openings like the pockmarks of a bloodsucking lamprey. With a shiver, the disappointed fisherman dropped the creature into his creel. If he had caught no salmon, still he had snagged a curiosity worth showing his kinsmen at Lambton Hall.

On his way back to the castle, the heir met an old servant, who greeted him and asked about his morning's sport. "Not a single salmon have I hooked," said the youth, "but, truly, I think I have caught the devil himself. Look in and judge." He opened the lid of the creel. The servant glanced in, and his face clouded. "It bodes no good," he said, lowering the lid and handing the basket back to his master. "This is evil come among us." Then he bade the boy good day and, shaking his head, hurried on. Uneasy, the young lord upended the creel over a roadside well's dank opening and tapped it until he heard a faint plop as the worm struck the water. Then he went on his way, oddly relieved.

Years passed uneventfully. Childe Lambton grew to manhood and, taking the Crusader's cross, sailed off to fight in the Holy Land. And deep in the dark, cold waters where it had landed, the

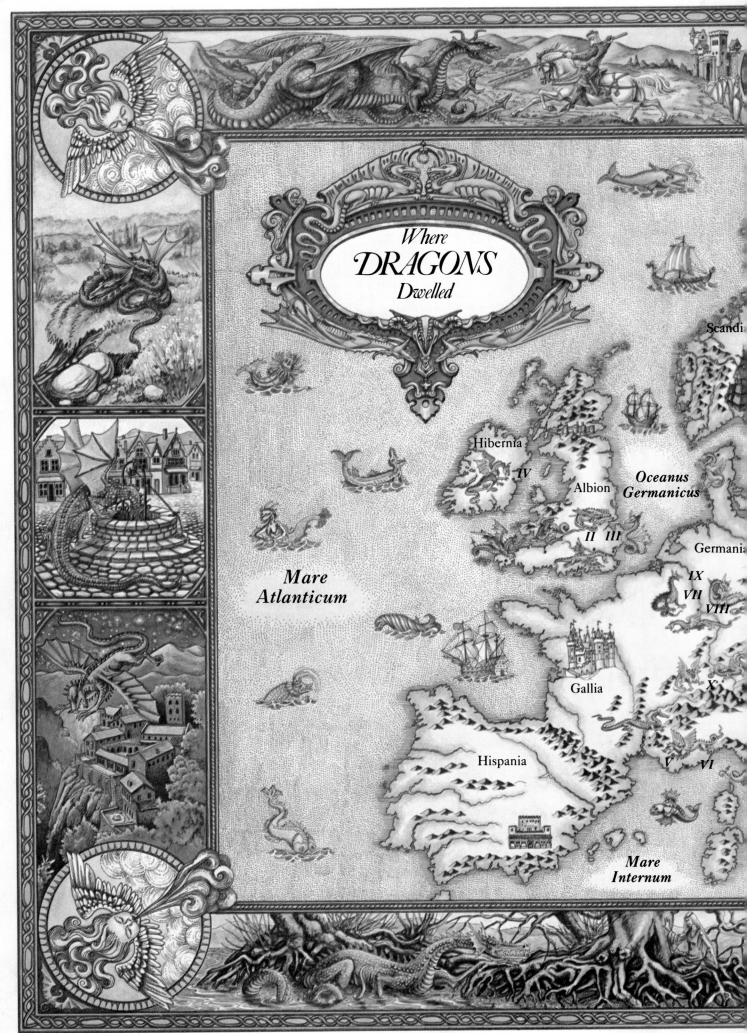

Where **DRAGONS** Dwelled

Scandi...

Hibernia

IV

Albion

Oceanus Germanicus

II III

Germani...

IX
VII
VIII

Mare Atlanticum

Gallia

X

Hispania

V VI

Mare Internum

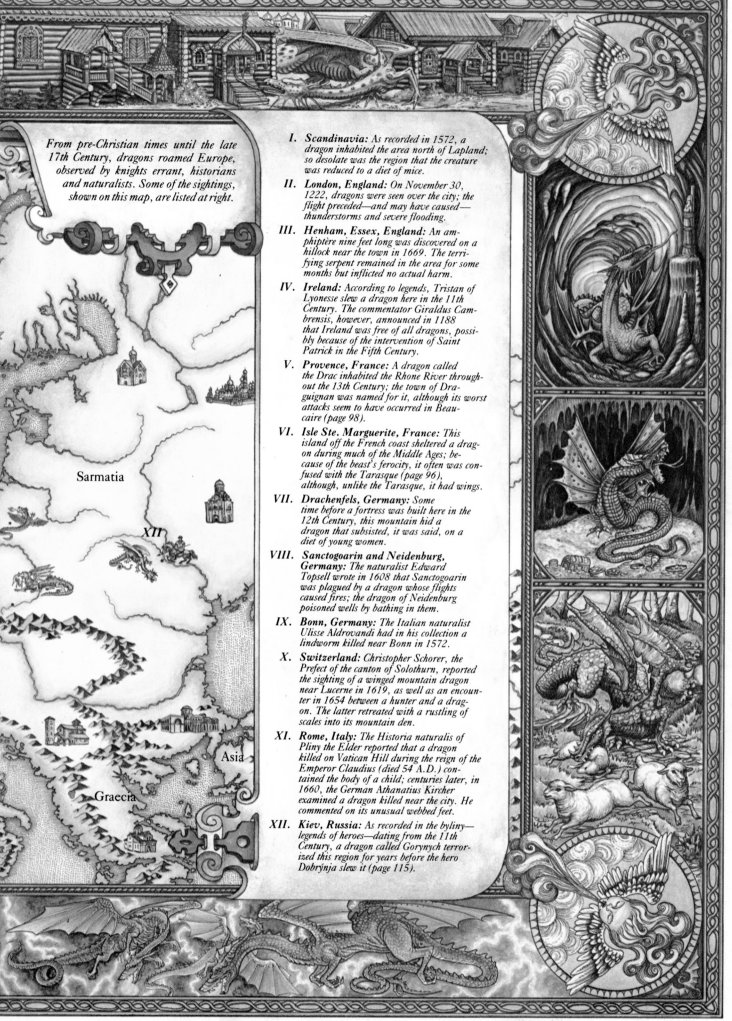

From pre-Christian times until the late 17th Century, dragons roamed Europe, observed by knights errant, historians and naturalists. Some of the sightings, shown on this map, are listed at right.

I. Scandinavia: *As recorded in 1572, a dragon inhabited the area north of Lapland; so desolate was the region that the creature was reduced to a diet of mice.*

II. London, England: *On November 30, 1222, dragons were seen over the city; the flight preceded—and may have caused—thunderstorms and severe flooding.*

III. Henham, Essex, England: *An amphiptère nine feet long was discovered on a hillock near the town in 1669. The terrifying serpent remained in the area for some months but inflicted no actual harm.*

IV. Ireland: *According to legends, Tristan of Lyonesse slew a dragon here in the 11th Century. The commentator Giraldus Cambrensis, however, announced in 1188 that Ireland was free of all dragons, possibly because of the intervention of Saint Patrick in the Fifth Century.*

V. Provence, France: *A dragon called the Drac inhabited the Rhone River throughout the 13th Century; the town of Draguignan was named for it, although its worst attacks seem to have occurred in Beaucaire (page 98).*

VI. Isle Ste. Marguerite, France: *This island off the French coast sheltered a dragon during much of the Middle Ages; because of the beast's ferocity, it often was confused with the Tarasque (page 96), although, unlike the Tarasque, it had wings.*

VII. Drachenfels, Germany: *Some time before a fortress was built here in the 12th Century, this mountain hid a dragon that subsisted, it was said, on a diet of young women.*

VIII. Sanctogoarin and Neidenburg, Germany: *The naturalist Edward Topsell wrote in 1608 that Sanctogoarin was plagued by a dragon whose flights caused fires; the dragon of Neidenburg poisoned wells by bathing in them.*

IX. Bonn, Germany: *The Italian naturalist Ulisse Aldrovandi had in his collection a lindworm killed near Bonn in 1572.*

X. Switzerland: *Christopher Schorer, the Prefect of the canton of Solothurn, reported the sighting of a winged mountain dragon near Lucerne in 1619, as well as an encounter in 1654 between a hunter and a dragon. The latter retreated with a rustling of scales into its mountain den.*

XI. Rome, Italy: *The Historia naturalis of Pliny the Elder reported that a dragon killed on Vatican Hill during the reign of the Emperor Claudius (died 54 A.D.) contained the body of a child; centuries later, in 1660, the German Athanatius Kircher examined a dragon killed near the city. He commented on its unusual webbed feet.*

XII. Kiev, Russia: *As recorded in the byliny—legends of heroes—dating from the 11th Century, a dragon called Gorynych terrorized this region for years before the hero Dobrýnja slew it (page 115).*

Sarmatia

XII

Asia

Graecia

worm grew and gathered strength. Passersby began to notice an eye-stinging vapor curling up from below, and villagers who, against prudent counsel, still filled their vessels at the well reported that the water caught in their throats and burned their skin.

One morning there was no longer need to speculate about what had tainted the well. Throughout the district, wayfarers and early-rising farmers pounded on cottage doors to warn of the evil that had arisen during the night. The well, they reported, was rimmed with glistening slime, and a broad trail of reeking muck led down the dusty lane to the river. There, draped over a rock in midstream, in coils as intricate as a Celtic brooch, was a dragon. The worm had grown into its maturity, and all who saw it fled before the threat in its eyes.

Like most English dragons, it lacked legs, wings and fire, but there was grisly power in its coils, in its fangs and in the chill spray of venom that misted its breath. That morning the dragon was at ease. But in the days that followed, its rapacity brought ruin to Lambton.

By day the dragon mounted the rock in the middle of the Wear; at night it retreated to the riverbank, where it twined itself three times around a knoll. When it slithered back to the river as the sun rose, the grassy flanks of the knoll were marked with a spiraling band of yellow where the monster's slime had blighted the turf. And whenever hunger seized it, day or night, the dragon went marauding. Herds panicked and fled when it loomed at the brow of a hill and then slipped liquidly down toward their pasture. Lambs, nibbling the tender grass that grows in low spots, were overcome as the monster's breath settled into the depressions, and they quickly fell prey to the dragon's voracity. Lumbering milch cows, too, were caught, but these it did not kill outright. Greedy for milk, it raked their udders with its fangs, cruelly injuring the animals.

While the dragon prowled, a pall of silence fell upon the district. In Lambton Hall, the old lord waited, safe behind stout ironbound gates. In the village, his villeins huddled in their cottages and his poor cotters in their fragile huts. The church door stood open and wind sang in the rafters, but the church was empty, for the priest had fled. The sails of the mill on the river were still; no miller was there to watch them. The only voices heard were those of injured cattle, lowing in the fields near the town. From time to time the dragon ventured into the village, its coils rasping and slithering in the narrow streets. No heads appeared at the windows to watch it, however, and it lost interest in the village.

At last the worm tired of the depleted herds and headed up the hill toward Lambton Hall. But the people in the castle had had time to think, and they were ready. An old steward, remembering dragons' love of milk, had kept the milkmaids busy in the cow byre. Bucket by bucket, he had poured warm, frothy milk into a horse trough outside the hall gates. Now, from the safety of the fortress, he watched the beast's laborious approach.

The dragon snaked up the hillside, wreathed in poisonous mist, making straight for the gates. It caught the odor of the milk and paused. Then it plunged its sleek head into the trough and drank long and deep. At last it lifted its head, now filmed with milk, from the empty trough and sluggishly shifted its coils down the hill toward its midstream retreat.

Thus began a ritual that was to last for years. The daily offering of milk transformed the dragon from a fierce marauder to a noxious parasite. With time, even the most fearful of the peasants emerged from their shuttered houses to hack the weeds from their untended fields and round up their scattered flocks. But the countryfolk all shunned the lane, its surface slick with venom, that had become the dragon's route between river and castle.

The humiliating truce dragged on for seven years. There were attempts to slay the dragon, but the would-be heroes lost their lives to its teeth and slashing claws. The district was freed only when Childe Lambton – he who all unknowing had given the beast a home among his people – returned from his distant campaigns.

He knew his duty then. It was later said that, clad in spiked armor, he met the dragon on its river rock and submitted to the deadly embrace of those coils. The spear points that bristled on the knight's breastplate pierced the dragon's hide, and the loss of blood weakened the dragon enough for the mortal to finish the job with his broadsword.

Lambton was freed. But the people were never again able to look at their orderly fields, tidy cottages, and the guardian presences of Lambton Hall and the village church and feel that their world was securely buttressed against disorder.

The sudden intrusion of a dragon into settled village life was only one of the guises in which chaos could shatter the seemly surface of mortal existence. But even when catastrophe took other forms, such as war, disease or famine, it was likely to be heralded by the sight of dragons roaming abroad. They were drawn to disaster, as if to the smell of human blood and anguish, even when they played no part in bringing on the calamity.

In Norway, for instance, dragons were most often seen flying as high as migrating birds, harmlessly distant from mortal dwellings. But when thunderous wingbeats and a spurt of orange flame in the night sky signaled the nearby flight of a dragon, villagers gazed upward in fear and wonder. For they were witnessing not just the greatest of beasts in all its majesty but also an omen of some future sorrow.

Like celestial signposts, flights of dragons marked turning points in history. In 793, the monks at the monastery of St. Cuthbert, on the steep, rocky island of Lindisfarne, off the east coast of England, were roused from their prayers and studies. A hiss, as if from a vast bonfire of green logs, cut through the roar of the surf on the shore far below. In windows, courtyards and colonnaded galleries, monks threw back their cowls to stare into a sky that was alive with dragons – an airborne festival of the great beasts. At play, the dragons soared and tumbled and romped, and their scales shimmered in iridescent colors under the weak northern sun.

The *Anglo-Saxon Chronicle* tells what followed: "Shortly after that, on the sixth day before the Ides of January, the ravaging of the heathen men destroyed God's church, at Lindisfarne, through rapine and slaughter." Slim silhouettes had appeared on the horizon, then resolved themselves into a fleet of Viking long ships, their crested prows mirroring the profiles of their dragon forerunners. Swarming up from the beach, the brawny invaders pillaged the monastery and the nearby village, then torched all that would burn and spattered the unyielding stone walls with the blood of slaughtered monks and peasants. It was the first Viking raid to touch the coast of England and a terrible foretaste of the centuries of suffering that followed.

The dragons that augured the attack were innocent. Dragons never strayed far from the scene of misfortune, but they were not always its begetters. And even when they did spawn calamity, dragons, like the other elemental forces that shaped human existence, were less malignant than unpredictable and unruly. Churchmen guessed that the devil sometimes clothed himself as a dragon, just as he had taken the guise of a serpent in the Garden of Eden. But most dragons were not known to show the devil's subtle and purposeful malevolence. Their ferocity was mindless, born of strength and boundless appetite.

In the Swiss Alps, the fierceness of dragons was as familiar as anywhere else in Europe. Seized with unaccountable fury, they rampaged in high Alpine valleys, triggering rockslides, flattening stands of fir, and sending high walls of water and debris surging down mountain streams into the villages clustered on the banks. Yet one Swiss freeman dwelled a season with dragons and lived to tell about it.

The man was a cooper, and he had ventured over the gentle shoulders of the mountains that enclosed his native valley to a neighboring forest of beech and oak, to gather wood for barrel staves. It was autumn, and the forest floor was ankle-deep in fallen leaves. The cooper soon strayed from the path as he searched for low-hanging oak branches to cut and load on his mule.

As night fell, he realized that he had lost his way. His eyes strained at the darkness for the glow of a hunter's fire or a charcoal burner's hearth. Branches lashed his face as he groped through the dark forest, and suddenly the ground steepened under his feet. He dropped the mule's tether, took another step—and lost his footing entirely, glancing off roots and jutting rocks as he tumbled to the bottom of a ravine. There the ground was sticky with mud and the air was heavy with an unfamiliar smell, savoring of dung and burning leaves. Exhausted, the cooper curled up at the base of the cleft and slept.

When the pale morning light filtered into the chasm, the cooper awoke, stiff from his fall. He gazed up at the narrow gash of sky between the walls of the ravine, higher and steeper than he could hope to climb, and he despaired. Then he heard the heavy sigh of a sleeping animal, so near and forceful that it stirred his hair. It was as hot as the breath of a furnace and it bore a whiff of sulfur. The gust seemed to have come from a cleft on the far side of the ravine, and the cooper bent to peer

(continued on page

Of Maidens and Dragons

Long years ago, when dragons roamed free throughout Europe and Asia, the stories of maidens who were sacrificed to them were commonplace: If a dragon harassed a city, for instance, a young woman would be chained to a rock or pillar outside the gates. Often, it was said, such an offering of tender flesh brought relief from further depredations by the beast. But the converse of maidens with dragons in those days was far more complex than such simple tales would indicate. The powers women might hold over dragons were great and strange, as the vignettes that follow illustrate. Some women of fairy power displayed a certain affection—or at least tolerance—for dragons. They kept the creatures in thrall, either to harness their powers for evil purposes or simply to render the creatures harmless. And the capture of a mortal maiden frequently led not to her death but to the defeat of the dragon that had captured her.

Safe in a scented palace hidden in Kiev, the Russian sorceress Marina kept a dragon for a companion and serpents for pets. It was her wont to seduce brave dragonslayers and change them into harmless magpies or pigs or oxen. Marina met her end when a hero seduced her in turn and—in the absence of her guards—beheaded her.

Once, on the coast of Germany, a King's daughter was captured by a sea dragon. She kept herself from harm by charming the beast to sleep until her rescuers arrived. It was said that the greatest stargazer in the world found her; the greatest thief in the world stole her away; and the greatest hunter in the world slew the dragon for her.

into the dimness. Then he recoiled. There, massively entwined in the shadows, heavy-lidded eyes nearly closed with winter torpor, were two dragons.

As he fell to his knees to pray for deliverance, one of the dragons rose from its stupor. Wings folded like paper fans, the dragon issued from the cavern in a torrent of scaly coils, supported on four short, clawed legs. It flicked its tail at the cooper. The tip wound about him, catching him in a choking embrace. The dragon regarded its captive for a moment through a glaucous eye, then released him and retired to its den, leaving the cooper weak-kneed with terror, but unharmed.

With little hope of rescue and none of escape, the cooper passed the winter in that ravine, in the company of the somnolent dragons. For food he plucked the mushrooms that grew where the damp walls of the chasm were warmed by the dragons' breath; for water he cupped his hands to collect trickling moisture. Unmolested, he lost his fear of the beasts, and one night when snowflakes pinwheeled into the ravine, the piercing cold emboldened him: He crept into the cave and wedged himself among the dragons' warm coils. One of the beasts twisted its head back to glance at him. But then, tolerant of the intrusion, it settled back to the floor of the cavern and let him be.

Thus the cooper passed that night and all of the cold nights to come, and when spring arrived and meltwater cascaded into the chasm, the dragons saved him once again. One morning he awoke alone and cold in the smoky den. Through the opening of the cave he heard a rush of wingbeats. He hurried out to see one of the dragons, membranous wings spread wide and tail lashing, rising up the narrow ravine into the bright morning. The other dragon also was ready to set off into the awakening world, and it sprawled on the mud, slowly unfolding its wings like an insect newly emerged from a cocoon. When at length the dragon took to the air, the cooper seized its tail, holding on tight as the beast thrashed in its struggle to become airborne.

At the lip of the ravine, the cooper cast loose and dropped lightly to the ground. He stood for a moment to watch the dragon rise, glittering in the sunshine. Then he searched for the path he had strayed from the preceding autumn. He followed it home, to tell his story to astonished townsfolk who had given him up for lost many months before, when his mule wandered back alone.

The cooper was fortunate in encountering the dragons in their winter somnolence. Although they bore him no malice, his fate might have been very different if hunger had seized them. Docile as their demeanor could sometimes seem, dragons were destructive beasts, whose nature it was to wreak havoc on the mortal world.

Their innate character is made particularly evident in tales of transformation: In the age when the world was shot through with magic, people sometimes were turned into dragons. But the transformations in the West were of a different nature from those of Asia, where the dragon form cloaked spirits of godlike power.

No matter how fine mortals might be, the spells that made them dragons turned them into predators, seemingly as soulless as crocodiles.

Like other dragons, these human-souled beasts embodied not just a physical menace but a sign that other threats lay nearby. For they were almost always the product of an evil spell, as was shown in the story of Childe Wynde:

The castle of Bamburgh, seat of the Kings of Northumberland, had a stern appearance in the best of times. It brooded on a granite outcropping at the end of a great sweep of beach, with a small village clinging to its base. But for a period, the natural austerity of the place deepened to grimness and palpable sorrow. This change began with the second marriage of a long-ago King.

He was an old man and a widower, and he had two children. His son, Childe Wynde, was fighting in a foreign war when the King remarried. His daughter, Margaret—both fair of face and full of grace—welcomed her father's new lady kindly.

The new wife, a coldly handsome woman of that country, was distant in her manner and, it was said, cruel-natured. She did not mingle freely at her own wedding feast but kept apart—behavior that earned her curious looks from the members of her husband's court. As the wine flowed and the songs began, it was clear that Margaret was a general favorite; unkind comparisons were made between the daughter and the wife. The new Queen said nothing; she bided her time.

That night, when the castle was still, the new Queen acted. As the King snored, heavy with wine, she stole out to the courtyard. There, in the moonlight, she whispered incantations and traced mystic symbols in the dust.

Some little time later, Margaret awoke in her chamber, aware of a foul taste in her mouth and a numb weight in her limbs. She was ravenous, hungrier than ever before in her life. Something flashed in the gloom. She gazed at it and distinguished a taloned claw clad in bright scales that caught the moonlight. When she drew herself up in terror, the claw jerked toward her. At this, she screamed. Her cry echoed as a throaty bellow. She rolled from the bed, and the great armored tail that now was hers thrashed and bludgeoned and reduced every fixture in the room to kindling. Finally, exhausted, the newborn dragon sprawled on the floor and slept.

The next day, the cheerful morning bustle of the castle was rent by screams and shouts. Crazed with hunger, the dragon that was Margaret surged out of her chamber, down the stairs and through the castle gate into the morning air. From the pastures below drifted the scent of grazing sheep, and the dragon sped down the hill and savaged the flocks. Sated, it coiled itself around a wind-worn pillar of rock called Spindlestone Heugh to bask in the morning sunshine.

The people were terrified. They sought the advice of sorcerers and thus discovered the treachery of the new Queen and the way to break her spell. "If you wish to see Margaret returned to her true shape and the Queen justly punished, send over the

seas for Childe Wynde," they were told.

All this was done, although the King, fatuous in his old age, refused to believe in his wife's evil. The dragon remained a fearsome and foul-smelling presence, but it left off harrying the flocks in return for a daily trough of milk. More than that the people could not do. They had no way of releasing the soul of Margaret from its scaly prison.

Far across the waves, word of the beast reached Childe Wynde. He assembled his companions and sailed for England in a boat built over a keel of rowan wood, known for its power against the forces of evil. But an enemy awaited the warriors, contrived by the power of the prescient Queen. When the toothed battlements of the castle rose into view, the company saw a dreadful sight: Skimming the wave crests toward the ship was a tribe of imps, as formless as shadows, almost invisible save for flashing teeth and glittering eyes. They circled and darted, batlike, around the mast top. Yet the power of the rowan-wood keel held fast; they could not harm the ship. At last, exhausted, the imps settled to the waves and watched, bobbing like flotsam, as the boat knifed past them toward shore.

Trapped in the skin of a dragon by enchantment, Margaret of Bamburgh was rescued when her brother returned from abroad. He restored her to mortal form with a kiss, then covered her with his cloak and rode to the castle to take revenge on her enchanter.

Again the Queen acted, alone in her chamber, weaving her spells. The dragon uncoiled itself from Spindlestone Heugh and lumbered down to the beach, reluctant to halt the boat, whose banners it recognized, but powerless to resist. It lurched into the surf and sculled itself out to sea with powerful sweeps of its tail, bearing down on the ship. With a crash that sent the men tumbling from their benches, the dragon rammed the prow. Twice Childe Wynde and his crew regained headway, and twice more the dragon stopped them. At last Childe Wynde ordered the boat about and headed away toward a cove far from the castle.

When the ship, unhindered, ground onto the shingle, Childe Wynde leaped from the prow with his archers close behind. Suddenly a squall of gulls burst from the sand hills behind the beach and a choking mist enclosed the men. A long, scaly snout thrust from the vapor, and Childe Wynde found himself regarded by an eye the size and color of a lemon, flickeringly veiled by a filmy lid.

Childe Wynde brandished his sword, for he did not know that he looked upon the prison of his sister. The archers tensed their bows. Then the dragon's maw gaped,

Bejeweled haunters of the Alps

In the Alpine region of France and the neighboring Swiss cantons lived a dragon called a vouivre, a name derived from the Latin *vipera*, or viper. The vouivre was a magnificent creature, as bejeweled as the fabulous treasures it was said to guard. Its scales sparkled like diamonds; it bore a crown of pearls; and in the center of its forehead was a blood red carbuncle that served as its single eye. The stone was so luminous that the dragon appeared to be wreathed in fire when it flew, and for centuries, French parents told their children that shooting stars marked the vouivre speeding across the night skies.

One night each year, the creature became vulnerable. It left its lair — which might be the ruins of a château or abbey, or a mountain grotto or fissure in the rock of the region — and flew to lakes and streams to bathe and drink. When it entered the water, it removed the precious red carbuncle and placed the stone on the ground. In this blinded state, the vouivre drank its fill.

There would seem to have been opportunity in this, and peasants of the region were fond of saying that anyone brave enough to approach the beast and steal the stone would be as rich as a king, while the vouivre, deprived of sight forever, would languish and die. But this was wishful thinking, for the fiery dragon thrived for centuries, and no tales survive of peasants profiting from its treasure.

93

and loosed a roar. In the depths of the tumult Childe Wynde heard Margaret's voice telling him the means of saving her.

The knight motioned off his men and slipped his sword into its scabbard. He knelt by the beast, whose breath blasted his cheek and stung his eyes. Twice he kissed the poison-dewed scales that fringed the fangs. Razor edges lacerated his mouth, but he gave a final kiss, and as his lips brushed the scales the dragon began to wither. Its eyes dimmed and its body curled and crumpled like a fallen leaf. Soon it was no more than a rigid yellow husk, a castoff shell. Then this, too, vanished, crumbling into evanescent flakes to reveal the unclothed form of a slender woman, her skin shining like a newborn's. It was Margaret, and Childe Wynde rushed forward to protect her from the sharp sea breeze with his cloak. Then, in the company of his men, brother and sister set off for the castle.

Jubilation erupted when they reached the castle, but the young man had more to do. He left his sister with her father and strode to the chamber of the witch-queen. Her power had vanished when the rowan keel of Childe Wynde's boat touched the sand, and he now found her huddled in a corner of her chamber. Her eyes were bright with terror as he drew from his pocket a rowan twig plucked from the same tree that was felled to make the keel. She shrank wordlessly as he stretched the twig toward her, but at its touch she shrieked. At once her cry grew choked and muffled, and abruptly it ended in a hoarse croak. Childe Wynde blinked, for the Queen's form had vanished. In its place, no higher than a man's ankle and as wrinkled as a raisin, squatted a toad.

Childe Wynde drew back at the sight, then began to laugh. As if fleeing his mockery, the toad hopped from the room and fled pell-mell down the steps to the dungeons. There the witch-queen wedged herself into a cleft in the dank wall, and nothing was ever heard of her again except an occasional croak, echoing faint and doleful through the deep galleries.

A few communities, like Bamburgh, were released by magic from the scourge of dragons; many more were saved by a bold dragonslayer. But people of those days also looked to another source of succor — to Christianity, which promised a universe in which dragons, creatures of riot, could have no place.

Christianity was the enemy of unbounded appetite, the animating principle of dragons. And its prayers and symbols, with their message of self-restraint and humility, had an extraordinary power over dragons, as is shown in a Cornish tale. The story took place in days when the people of Cornwall still clung to heathen ways. Drawn to the challenge of winning them for the faith, an energetic saint named Samson journeyed among them, preaching and healing and performing miracles. The greatest of these involved a dragon, a great glossy serpentine beast that dwelled in a cave by a stream on the side of a moorland valley.

The ravages of the dragon had left the district backward and poor, and the countryfolk led the wonderworking saint to the valley and begged him to turn his magic—for so it seemed to them—against the beast. While the tattered band of peasants waited nervously on the far side of the dale, the saint picked his way across the stream and entered the cave, calling for the dragon. With a hiss it shot from its shadowy lair. Even as its fangs sliced toward him, the saint intoned holy words. At once the serpent's body went limp. The chroniclers report that the dragon vented its last spasm of ferocity on itself, doubling back and gnawing its own tail.

The saint then looped his linen belt around the dragon's neck and, before the astonished crowd, led the docile creature out of the cave. Vast and spiritless, it slithered beside him across hill and gully to the cliffed shore. At the dizzy edge of the cliff the saint halted. He prodded the dragon with his staff until it inched forward and slipped over the precipice, plunging to its death in the shallows. Surf surged around its inert bulk as it lay sprawled on the rocks, while far above, peering down from the cliff top, the countryfolk rejoiced.

Other saintly subduers of dragons showed more mercy. Refusing to view the beasts as intrinsically more evil than any other natural creature, they forgave the vanquished dragons their trespasses. A Cornish saint named Carantoc soothed a swamp-dwelling monster with prayer, then led the beast into the wilderness and, with words of admonition, left it there to pursue its dragonish ways far from mortal dwellings. Saint Petroc, in a similar display of loving-kindness, subdued the last Cornish dragon by whispering a psalm in its ear. He then conducted the beast to the

The serpent and the Cross

In the face of Christianity, dragon power began to wane, or so the Christian legends said. They told, for instance, of Margaret, an early believer who lived in Antioch. The governor of the city, a pagan named Olybus, fell in love with the young woman, but she repulsed all his advances, even though he had her cast in prison for the refusals. A dragon threatened her in her prison cell, according to the legends, but fled when she held a wooden cross up before its eyes. Other versions of this saint's tale claim that the dragon actually swallowed the woman and that the cross she bore grew inside it until the beast was split asunder. Margaret stepped safely from its belly, and because of this deliverance she became the patron saint of childbirth.

shore and commanded it to take to the water, to seek some deserted island for its new home. Accepting banishment, the dragon swam out toward the horizon and was lost to view.

But a merciful saint could not always restrain the long-suffering population from taking revenge on a dragon. When a region was finally relieved of the scourge, the people, able at last to express their rage and resentment, often rose up as one against the beast. That was the fate of a dragon named the Tarasque, the terror of a district in the South of France near the town then known as Nerluc.

Descriptions of dragons rarely are reliable, for those who encountered a dragon were usually so frightened that they seized on a single grisly feature without taking note of the beast as a whole. Confused as they are, though, records of the Tarasque suggest an exceptional dragon. Unlike its northern cousins, the Tarasque was hulking rather than sinuous—a small mountain of flesh clad in armor-plate scales and sup-

Rapacious and cunning, the lion-headed Tarasque brought horror to the farms of Provence. No animal was safe from its appetite until a young saint named Martha challenged it with the power of her faith.

ported on six stout legs. It could destroy fields and dwellings by fire, which issued in streams from its mouth, or by flood, which it caused by lashing the waters of the Rhone River with its tail. During its roamings through fields and olive groves and vineyards, it devoured beasts and herdsmen alike.

The well-armored Tarasque was impervious to the sharpest weapons that smiths could forge, wielded by the stoutest champions of Nerluc. But hope of relief from its depredations stirred when a fresh-faced girl, clad in a dress of white linen, docked her small boat at the harbor of the town.

Her name was Martha, and she was a saint. The fame that had gathered about her good deeds and simple preaching in Arles, a city to the south, had preceded her, and the townsfolk beseeched her for aid against the Tarasque. She did not quail but set off alone into the deserted fields beyond the town walls, guided by the tang of smoke and the baaing of frightened sheep.

She reached a meadow, once verdant but now an expanse of charred stubble. Through the smoky pall loomed the form of the Tarasque itself. It gulped the last of a bloody carcass and, snorting with satisfaction, wheeled to face Martha. She picked up two blackened straws; then, a fragile figure in white, she strode up to the mighty Tarasque, crossed the sticks in the emblem of her faith and brandished them in its face. The dragon gave a great sigh and slumped to the ground, and its fierce eyes glazed over. Martha slipped a vial of holy water from her belt, opened it and sprinkled the Tarasque to complete her triumph.

By then its mouth was hanging open feebly, and the fearless child bent her head against one of its fangs and snipped off her long braids, one by one. She knotted them together to form a tether, looped it around the Tarasque's neck and set off for town with the dragon shuffling beside her, its tail dragging in the dust.

When the people of Nerluc gathered in the square to wonder at the saintly maiden and her conquest, they were at first disbelieving, then fearful and finally seized by a fierce joy. Martha pleaded for the beast's life as she saw the crowd begin to pry up stones and clods. But there was little she could do against the fury that burst forth. The unresisting Tarasque was spat upon and pelted and even, as the mob gained confidence, pummeled with bare fists. The dragon drew in its head like a tortoise and sank slowly to the dirt. At last, with an expiring puff of yellow smoke, it died.

Many other dragons met violent ends, although most fell to bold and resourceful dragonslayers rather than to the rages of mobs. But no town or country district that had felt the fury of a dragon could soon forget the oppressor. Shortly after the Tarasque's demise, the town of Nerluc, in a solemn ceremony, took the name by which it is now known: Tarascon. It was also decreed that the town seal should bear an image of the great dragon so that later generations might know what tribulations the town had suffered and how fragile are the works of human beings before the primordial forces of nature.

Sojourn in a Watery Realm

Through the vineyards and olive groves of southern France, past the amber castles of the lords of Provence and the red-roofed villages of their vassals, rolled the River Rhone, and the stately sweep of its waters gave no sign that it sheltered dragons. One dwelled in its depths, however: Near the town of Beaucaire, where the Rhone curved down toward the sea, was hidden the lair of the Drac, a huge and ancient creature wise in sorceries, which he used for his own bloody ends.

The Drac liked the taste of human flesh and took pleasure in hunting mortals. From time to time he left his river for the marketplace of Beaucaire, where, invisible to the busy townsfolk, he loitered in the shade of the plane trees, a watchful shadow among the baskets of fish and mounds of fruit. With cold, pale eyes, the dragon observed the housewives of the town as they chattered with the tradesmen; with swift, curving claws, he snatched away any untended child.

Sometimes for sport, on the other hand, the Drac lured mortals into his river and trapped them there. He did so once for a curious purpose, and this is how it happened:

One summer afternoon, when the sun beat hot on the town and fields, a young wife of the town went to the river to wash her infant's clothes. As she worked, the woman glanced idly at the sparkling water – and then she stared. Floating on the

surface just offshore was a golden cup. In the rich vessel shone a single pearl.

With scarcely a thought, she took the lure. She stretched her hand out to grasp the pretty bauble, but the cup bobbed just out of reach, glittering seductively in the sunlight. She reached again, leaning far out from the riverbank, and thus she lost her balance.

She fell, and as she fell, a claw struck out, a manacle that tightened at once around the mortal wrist. The young woman gasped and struggled, but she was helpless in that grasp. She felt a powerful downward drag. As her skirts filled with water, she saw a last image of the land—small clothes drying on the grass beside the river, the infant wailing all alone. Then the Rhone closed above her head.

Inexorably she was drawn down into the river's cold depths, until all she saw was watery blackness, broken by tiny lights, bright and sparkling as stars in the night sky. She fainted.

She opened her eyes at last to find herself in a cavern of crystal. Outside its translucent walls, water reeds danced slowly as if blown by a land wind. Fish darted by. Near her, within the walls, lay the golden cup that had tempted her and the pearl that it had held. And then she saw her captor. Vast and gleaming, the dragon crouched motionless beside the cup, steadily regarding her.

Lost in its green gaze, the woman rose to her feet, and as she did so, the memory of her life in France faded: Her infant son, her husband, her house in sunny Beaucaire, the fields and olive groves around the town, all became tiny images, miniature pictures remembered vaguely, as dreams are remembered. Only the dragon's words sounded in her head. The Drac spoke with a voice that echoed like a gong, and the mortal obeyed.

The Drac had lured and trapped the woman because she was young and healthy—and because she was the nursing mother of a baby son. The dragon needed mortal milk to sustain his own hatchling, a small and fragile dragon spawn. So the young woman, caught in a net of enchantment, became the slave of the Drac and the nurse to a dragon.

Days passed peacefully, and for the mortal captive in the dim twilight of the crystal cave beneath the river, one day was much like another. Lulled by the motion

of the water outside and by the dragon spell, she lived as if in a trance. She suckled the hatchling of the Drac and cared for its other needs as tenderly as if it had been her own son. She slept when the Drac bade her and ate what he gave her. She watched the movement of the river through the opalescent walls of the cavern, and in time the creatures of the Rhone—the pike with its green and gold stripes, the twisting eels, the darting trout—became as familiar to her as the villagers of Beaucaire once had been. As each day passed, she saw the watery world that enveloped her more clearly and more intimately, as if the rocks and reeds were the fields and woods of her own forgotten home.

Ber vision came from dragon magic, although she did not know this. Each night, as she was ordered, she anointed the hooded eyes of the hatchling with a salve the Drac gave her. The salve endowed the infant with a dragon's piercing sight, and whenever the woman happened to rub her own eye, a little of the ointment lodged there, so that she received something of the creature's magical power.

Seven years passed. The hatchling grew large and strong, and the day came when the Drac had no further use for his captive. He did not kill her as he might have done, for she had nourished his own offspring. Instead, he released her, setting on her spells of forgetfulness and sleep before he bore her up through the river and into the daylight.

The woman awoke on the riverbank near her own home. She looked around in some confusion, for her recollection was of a hot and sunny day when she had washed her white linens and laughed at her infant as he played on the grass. But now the sun had set and the lights of the town were winking on one by one. Neither the linens nor her baby was anywhere to be seen. She hurried across the fields and through the streets of her town.

The door of her house stood open to the cool of the evening, and the woman walked in. Two half-familiar faces turned to her—a bearded man and a boy who resembled her husband in his youth. For a moment she stared at them and they at her. Then the man leaped to his feet with a sharp cry. While the boy watched wide-eyed, the man embraced her. He was her husband, who had thought her drowned

103

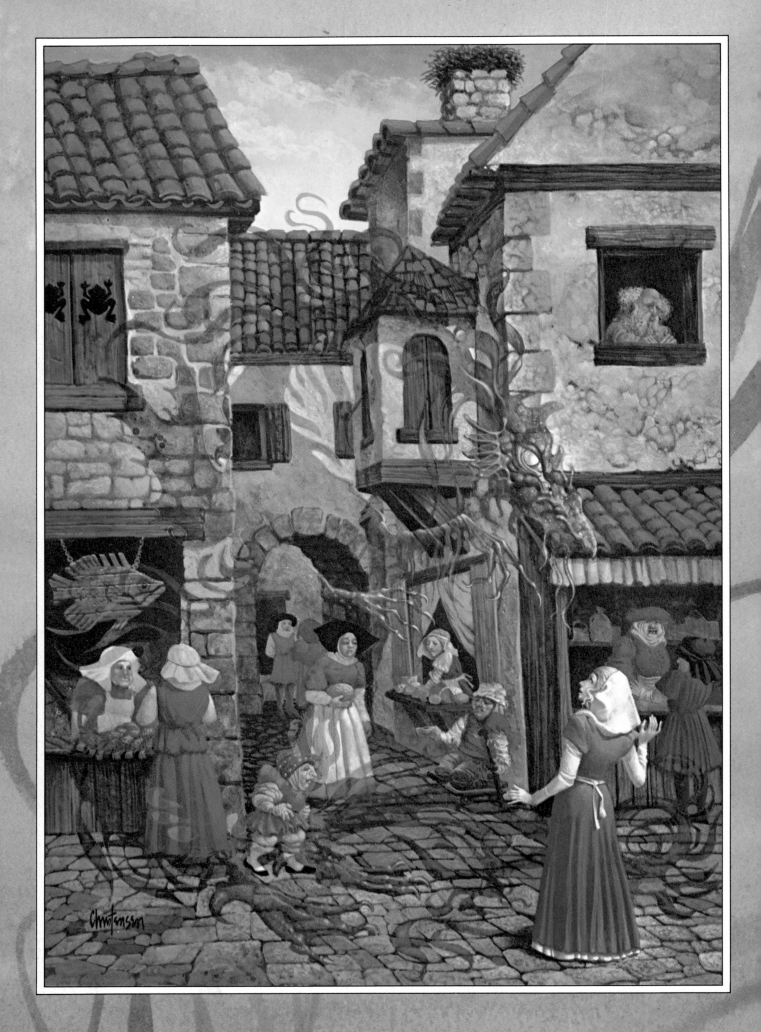

and had mourned faithfully for seven years. He plied her with questions, but she could give no answers, for she had no memory of the dragon's world. The young boy was her own son, but he spoke not at all to the white-faced, ragged stranger. She alarmed him by her silence.

Still, the father's love of his wife was so strong and his joy in her return so great that the son came to accept the stranger. So, too, did her neighbors in the weeks that followed her strange reappearance. Her seven years' absence remained a mystery to them, and her talk sometimes frightened them: She dreamed of dragons, she often said. But her neighbors were kindly people, and they let the woman be. She settled into the orderly, placid pattern of her early life, cooking and taking care of the man and the boy, and working with the townsfolk in the fields.

She would have continued thus, save for the dragon sight. One day she went to the marketplace, as was her habit, and there among the vegetable vendors and fishmongers she saw the Drac. Scaled and shining, he loomed above the townsfolk. His mighty head reached almost to the rooftops and his eyes glowed green, but the busy merchants and those who bought their wares went unknowing about their business. Only the woman saw him. When she cried out, he looked sharply at her.

"You see me, mortal?" asked a voice in her head.

"I see you, dragon," she said aloud, and at that moment she remembered all of her seven lost years.

She stood motionless as the dragon claw descended and covered her left eye.

"Do you see me now?" said the dragon voice. Still she saw him. The claw moved to cover her right eye, and where the dragon had stood she saw only the marketplace and her neighbors. Obediently, she told the Drac that she no longer saw him. Instantly her head was pierced with blinding pain. The claw had put out the eye that had the dragon sight.

The woman lived on, half-blind, for many years, and she told her dragon tale over and over. The villagers thought her mad and ignored her pitiful warnings. Thus, year after year, children continued to disappear from the marketplace, and no one ever knew the reason why.

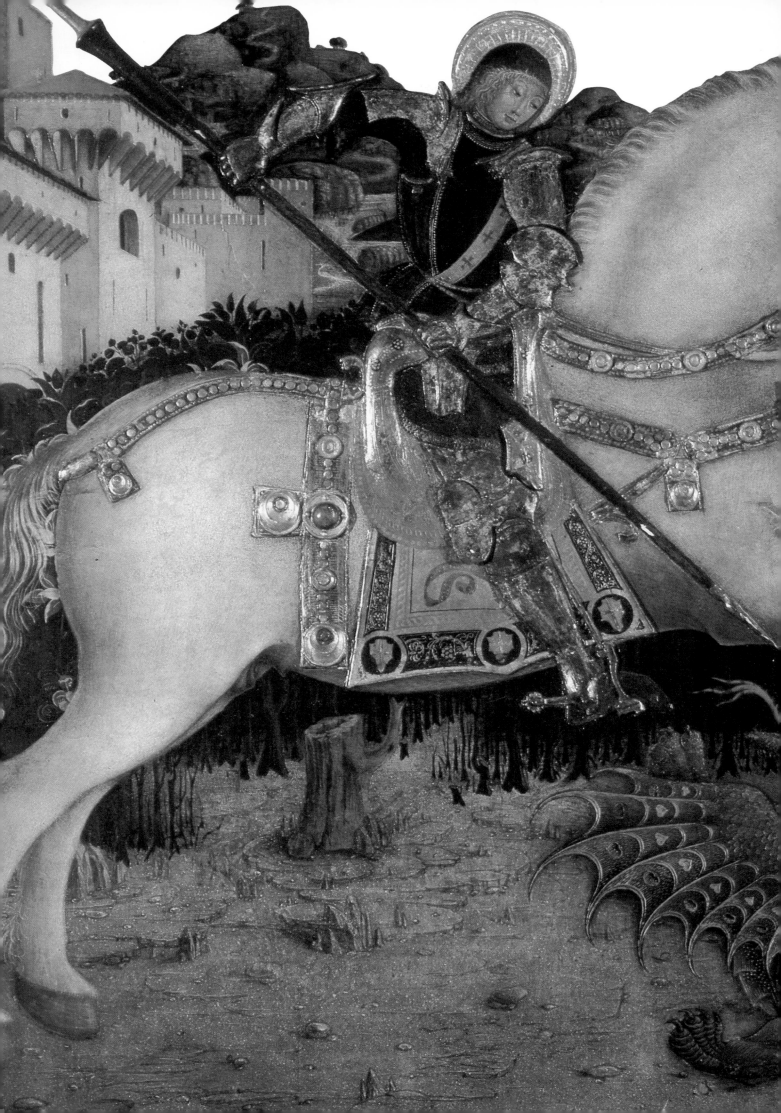

Chapter Four

Rise of the Dragonslayer

In an age abrim with valiant deeds, dragon fighters — men and women who vanquished the mighty beasts one by one — established an unmatched standard of courage. And among that glorious company of warriors, Saint George was the nonpareil. Clad in silver armor, riding a horse caparisoned in gold and always displaying the sign of the Christian — a red cross on a white field — he galloped through the stories and songs of the European lands, the harbinger of Christianity and its civilizing order, and the hammer of the dragon race. The fame of this soldier-saint was such that for centuries after his death, he was claimed as the protector of England, Catalonia, Aragon, Italy and Greece, and revered in such diverse parts as Lithuania, Portugal and Constantinople. In England his feast day, April 23, was a national holiday, celebrated with splendid processions, with pageants and plays. And England's highest honor, the Order of the Garter, was established in his name.

Saint George was the patron of all who had to do with battle — knights, archers, saddlemakers and swordsmiths. And he was the special guardian of the Crusaders as they fought the Saracens: It was said that he appeared with a mighty spirit host at the Battle of Antioch in 1098 and again in a blaze of light at the Battle of Jerusalem the following year, both times giving heart and victory to the weary Christian warriors. The battle cry of the Crusaders was the name of Saint George.

Yet who was he? Few knew, for a panoply of legends shone around him: He was said to have slain dragons at Mansfeld in the center of Germany; he was also said to have killed a dragon in England, in Berkshire, where the people pointed to a place called Dragon Hill, made grassless and barren by the venomous blood of his victim. Yet the first account of Saint George's slaying of a dragon is set not in Europe at all, but far south, in Africa. It happened this way:

In the early centuries of the present era, when Romans could justly call the Mediterranean *Mare Nostrum* – Our Sea – the province of Libya was a settled and urbane part of the far-flung Roman Empire. The province was long and narrow, hemmed in by the salt water of the Mediterranean and the sandy wastes of the Sahara. Yet Libya was richly productive. Fields of barley and wheat flowed into one another, forming a ribbon of grain that stretched unbroken for hundreds of miles and provided plenteous harvests to stock the imperial granaries. Cattle and sheep fattened on the surplus grain or grazed on the wild grass that grew in the valleys along the edge of the desert, where no crops could be cultivated.

The chief city of the province was called Silene, and for centuries it flourished along with the land, ruled by petty kings, who willingly paid the Romans tribute for the sake of peace. But a conqueror worse than the legions of Rome eventually blighted the city's calm and prosperity.

It was a savage dragon, sprung from somewhere in the bleak hills that divided the fertile coastal plain from the desert, and it settled in a marsh not far from the walls of the city.

The evidence of its presence appeared only gradually. Mangled carcasses of sheep and cattle were occasionally found in remote pastures; from time to time, also, the bloated corpses of travelers and shepherds were seen lying at the edge of the desert. Then the deaths began to happen closer to home, near the villages and hamlets that lay on the outskirts of the city. Children died, and the cows in their byres and the sheep in their pens. In Silene, whispers began. The curfew was rung early in the evenings, and the great gates were closed. Few people were so reckless as to stay outside the walls at night.

The dragon was thus deprived of easy game. But when it struck Silene, it came in broad daylight. A watchman at the gate felt the ground shudder; he squinted into the distance and saw the slouching beast, its scales shining in the African sun, trails of smoke curling around its head, and he gave the alarm. The gates were closed and barricaded. People crowded the walls as the armored serpent approached – on massive legs tipped with curving claws.

The dragon did not attack at once. It slithered around the base of the walls, nosing at crevices, trying its strength on the gates. The gates held, however. High on the walls, the watching people of the city stirred and sighed. But then, the dragon threw back its great head and howled. A spurt of foul-smelling, flaming liquid shot from the cruel mouth, snaked up the walls and poured over the battlements. The citizens who had gathered there were bathed in the caustic liquid. Writhing and screaming, they fell from the walls. The dragon devoured them on the spot.

That was the beginning of a time of terror. The city was besieged: Every day the dragon clawed at the gate and spewed its noxious venom over the ramparts. Outside the walls, the villages were silent and the fields untended; all the farmers had fled or been killed by the beast. Inside the city, people kept to their houses. The streets were empty, the markets vacant, the squares deserted. And no one ventured forth in an attempt to slay the creature, for its poison killed agonizingly and quickly. Sword and lance were useless against it.

Casting about for a means of appeasement, the King who ruled Silene decreed that two sheep be tied up outside the walls as a daily offering. The tactic seemed to work at first. Each day at dawn, soldiers led the sheep to a stake outside the gates and tied them there. The men then retreated and stood shivering behind the ramparts with the rest of the citizenry as the dragon claimed its gift with a horrible crunching of bones and smacking of lips. Well fed, the beast left Silene alone. But the day came when the city had no more sheep to offer, and the dragon began to circle the walls ceaselessly, spewing its deadly venom at any living target.

And thus began the lottery. Every day in the chill hour before the dawn, the people of Silene gathered in the square before the King's palace. From a great brass urn, they drew ivory counters that in happier times had been used for gambling. But this gamble was desperate, for the one who lost by drawing a marked counter was condemned to die so that the rest of the citizenry might live one more day. Wailing and lamentation arose in the dusty square as the victim's name was revealed. That person was tied to the stake outside the gates, just as the sheep had been, and died no less cruelly.

One morning, the marked counter fell to the daughter of Silene's King. The crowd—now much reduced by the daily sacrifice—moved away from the ruler and his child. The King stood motionless, a man turned to stone. He shook his head from side to side, and tears coursed down his face. But when the people began to murmur, he bowed in assent, and two of his guards moved toward the Princess.

They led her into the palace, and there her maidens clothed her all in white, as if to meet a bridegroom. Then they took her through the quiet streets, out to the slaughter ground. In that charred and bloodied landscape, among the bleaching bones of earlier victims, the soldiers bound her to the stake and left her to die.

But while the beast still slept in its lair, a man on horseback appeared on the eastern horizon, just ahead of the rising sun. Its rays struck his silver armor and formed a nimbus of light around his body as he rode toward the Princess, across the withered and treeless fields where no birds sang to greet the day. He was George, a Roman knight—but a Christian, as the red crosses on his sword belt showed. He was riding abroad in search of adventure, and he had come to the place of his trial. He drew rein beside the Princess and bent from his saddle to hear her tale.

The Princess begged the knight to leave her to her death. He only laughed—a strong and joyous sound in that place—and wheeled his horse toward the dragon's

Saint George, valorous and pure of heart, slew a dragon to rescue a Princess of Libya. His reward—say some legends—was the hand of the maiden he had saved.

den. The hoofbeats roused the beast, and it sprang screaming from the lair, head thrown back to spit venom and fire. But the knight was upon it before it could draw breath. As it reared to strike, his lance pierced its side, and the poison from its jaws trickled harmlessly to the ground. The knight moved in for the kill.

How the dragon died is a matter of debate. That the knight killed it, all chronicles grant. But some accounts say that he gave the death blow on the spot, while others declare that he cut the sign of the Cross into the wounded creature's belly and led the dragon back into Silene. There he demanded as payment the conversion of the people to Christianity, and when the religion was accepted, he struck off the dragon's head. It was said, too, that the Princess became the bride of her rescuer.

Whatever the precise shape of these events, the Christian knight who championed the new order of the world slew the avatar of the old. Yet the elder faiths and the old disorder did not vanish at once. George himself was martyred by pagans for his faith, according to some chronicles. (The tales of his death record a devastation as bad as any dragon's: He was said to have been tortured for seven days with knives, with breaking of bones and with live burial in quicklime.) And many more dragonslayers would follow him before the world was safe for humankind.

Many had preceded him, of course: The battle between the creatures of chaos and those of mortal order was old indeed. The first gods — Marduk and Zeus, Apollo and Thor — all battled dragons at the beginning of time. And their mortal progeny — the men who trod the earth at its dawn — had to fight the great beasts again and again.

The chief reward of fighting a dragon was an undying glory that kept a name alight in the hearts of humankind long after the hero himself had gone to dust. Indeed, the names of the great dragonslayers — Perseus and Hercules, Saint George himself, Sigurd the Volsung — rang bravely across whole millennia. Alexander the Great was reputed to have slain dragons; in fact, his fighting prowess and courage were such that he was said to have been sired by one, although most creditable scholars claimed only that, on the night before she bore him, his mother dreamed that she had given birth to a dragon.

There were more rewards than fame. Dragonslayers won from the blood of the beasts such ancient knowledge as an understanding of the languages of birds and animals, and such gifts as invulnerability to wounds. Many — like Saint George and Perseus — found wives as a result of their

conquests. Many won fabulous hoards of treasure, as Beowulf and Sigurd did.

But rewards, whether glory or riches or magic power, were not of central importance in understanding the age of the dragonslayer, although they may have motivated individual dragonslayers. These warriors most often fought to rid the land of an unbearable burden, to drive out the foe and thus ensure survival for themselves and their own. It was as if the creatures that remained from the beginnings of the world no longer belonged to it. They poisoned the earth and air; they made the fields sterile; they devoured the livestock that nourished humankind; they slaughtered mortals. Dragons thus had to be destroyed themselves.

Not all dragons were destroyers. Some were the stationary, solitary guardians of the waters from which they sprang and of the elemental treasures of the earth. But these were things that mortals needed or desired, and so the elder guardians of the world had to perish along with dragons that marauded.

Some of the guardian dragons, the dangerous worms of legend, laired in remote Welsh glens and fathomless Scottish lochs, seldom seen but much feared by fishermen. Others lived in Irish lakes and rivers, fiercely protecting remnants of an older world. Such a one once dwelled in Connacht, guarding a magical tree. The dragon was discovered by a Prince, in the course of a journey that was undertaken not for adventure but to secure a wife. What he found instead was betrayal.

The desperate combat of Lancelot

Lancelot of King Arthur's court once slew a dragon – and thereby set great events in motion. Here is the tale:

In a tomb in the part of France where King Pelles ruled, a dragon made its home. Each night it ventured out to maim and slaughter. When Lancelot reached that kingdom on his travels, the people begged for his aid. The gallant Lancelot went to the tomb and opened it; the dragon surged out upon him, but he slew the beast.

Inscribed upon the tomb were these words: "Here shall come a leopard of king's blood, and he shall slay this serpent. And this leopard shall engender a lion in this foreign country, which lion shall surpass all other knights." King Pelles knew of the inscription. He had a daughter named Elaine, and he believed that if Lancelot lay with her, she would bear the child who would become the knight of the prophecy.

But Lancelot loved Arthur's Queen Guinevere and would not lie with another lady. So by means of enchantment, Pelles gave Elaine the form of Guinevere. She invited Lancelot to her chamber in the evening, and he went willingly. Nine months later, Elaine bore Galahad, who, true to the foretelling, became the greatest warrior in all of Christendom.

The Prince was named Fróech, and he was only half mortal. His mother was a Princess of the Tuatha Dé Danann, the ancient fairy race that once ruled Ireland. By the time of this tale, the Tuatha had long since disappeared to underworld kingdoms, living in uneasy truce with the humans who had conquered the land.

The Prince, who dwelled among his mortal kin, showed his ancestry in his unearthly beauty, bravery and grace: "Of the heroes of Erin and of Alba," wrote a chronicler, "the most beautiful man was he, save only that he was short-lived." Fróech was tall and broad-shouldered, with hair as dark as a blackbird's wing and eyes the color of the mist that clung to the mountain ridges of Connacht. He kept a young man's court, with fifty princes like himself.

The ruler of Connacht at that period was Maeve, a warrior Queen who was as greedy for men as she was for battle. She maintained a ferocious and intermittent warfare with the province of Ulster and demanded that her husbands—of whom there had been several—be brave, generous and completely devoid of jealousy. Usually, however, there was much that was unfortunate in her mates' characters as well. One such husband was Ailill, a thoroughly underhanded man.

Strangely, this distasteful couple had a beautiful and generous-spirited daughter, Findabair. She heard tales of Fróech's handsomeness and strength and began to pine for him, sight unseen.

Word of her yearning came to the young man, for news traveled quickly in those days, carried by peddlers and bards who traveled from court to court.

The Princess was a prize indeed, and Fróech determined to ask for her hand. He set out for the plain of Cruachan. In the midst of the plain was Maeve's fortress, crowning a grassy mound called the Hill of Rathcroghan.

Maeve's watchman was the first to see the host of Fróech, and his cries of wonder brought the Queen's soldiers running. Fróech and his men displayed all the magnificence of the sons of the Tuatha. Their mantles were blue with clasps of red gold; their tunics were white, embroidered with golden animals. Their shields were chased silver; their lances gleamed with precious stones; they rode matching gray steeds, and the hounds that frolicked among them were collared in chains of silver hung with golden apples. And it was clear at once that Fróech's company came in peace: Yellow-haired jesters danced before the host; and walking gravely at the rear were three tall harpers, their instruments protected by bags of otter skin buckled with rubies.

The watchman saluted them all; they gave their names and were admitted to the courtyard of the fortress, where Maeve and Ailill waited. The Queen stood tall beside her little King, her glinting hair falling to her waist. On her shoulders perched two golden birds, which, it was said, gave her secret counsel, for Maeve was thought to have magical powers. Fróech knelt to greet the Queen. She regarded him closely as she gave the expected welcome.

Indirection was the custom then, so Fróech did not announce his purpose in coming to the Queen. His men hung up their arms in the outer court of the castle and joined the royal company. For two weeks they remained as guests, hunting and hawking in the fields around the fortress during the long summer days. At night they feasted in the firelit royal hall, listening to the harpers' music. Night after night, Fróech challenged the Queen at chess, knowing that she would not resist: If she could not have real battle, Maeve liked warfare with gold and silver men.

As they played, the Queen watched the Prince from under her lashes, for he aroused her desire. It mattered not to her that she had a lover at court as well as a husband: What attracted her, she took. But Fróech had come for the daughter, not the mother. He treated the Queen with deference, nothing more.

During that time, although the Prince waited patiently and occupied himself with the pleasures of the court, Findabair never appeared. Finally he found her: He rose just after dawn one day to bathe in the river that ran near the fortress, and there among the rushes was Findabair with her maid. Maeve's daughter was as rosy and sparkling as the summer dawn itself, and the chroniclers said that Findabair and Fróech loved each other from that moment. Some said that Findabair gave the Prince a golden ring that morning; all agreed that Fróech later returned to the audience hall in the fortress, where the King and Queen sat in conference, and asked for the maiden's hand.

The Queen looked at Fróech impassive-ly and stroked the bird that rode her shoulder. She said nothing, although flames burned in her cheeks, for she did not care to find a rival in her own child. She whispered to the King at length. Then Ailill gave his answer. "You may have my daughter in return for a purchase price," said the little King.

"You shall have it," replied the Prince.

But the price the King set was preposterous; he asked for the treasures of the Prince's fairy kin. He demanded sixty gray steeds with bridles of gold and twelve of the enchanted milk cows of the Tuatha Dé Danann, each with a white red-eared calf. Ailill demanded that Fróech commit all his forces to himself and the Queen: They would make strong allies for the battles Maeve was planning.

Fróech refused. "I would not pay that price for Maeve herself," he said. The Queen's lips tightened: Although his words at least placed her ahead of her daughter, Maeve was a woman used to more gallantry than that. The Prince then strode from the hall.

There were other ways to get a wife at that time. One was simply to steal her away from her parents, a common practice. Fróech knew that, and Maeve and Ailill knew it as well. They conferred after the Prince had left them. "If he steals Findabair," said the King, "he surely will join your enemies and march with their host against us. We are safest if we kill him now."

"It would dishonor us to slay an unarmed man," said Maeve.

"Such a thing could be done without loss of honor," replied Ailill, and he told

(continued on page

114

The Terror of Kiev

When white-halled Kiev was Russia's greatest
fortress-city, the land was rich in heroes, but few were of
the mettle of Dobrýnja Nikitich, who dared to
bargain with a dragon. His tale was this:
Not many days' ride from Kiev, bordering a
river-ribboned plain, rose the mountains of Sorochinsk,
known as a serpents' lair. The plain was dragon
country, domain of the many-headed, many-
tailed Gorynych, a fearsome predator that long
had menaced Kiev. Rarely did anyone set foot on that
plain. But one day a young man, gaily clad
and handsomely mounted, appeared beside
the river, riding briskly along the bank. This was
Dobrýnja, come to tempt the dragon.

He rode beside the river for several hours, but nothing stirred on the flat
expanse or in the mountains beyond on that hot summer
day. Finally, Dobrýnja dismounted, setting his horse free to graze.
He stripped off his clothes and dived into the water. At
once he heard a roaring in the distance and saw something streak like
a comet from the mountaintops; it was the enemy he sought.
The dragon landed on the riverbank, tails lashing, heads waving.
Dobrýnja leaped ashore to meet it. He filled his cap with
sand to make a weapon, using it to bludgeon the beast. In his battle fury,
he tore away three of the dragon's tails with his bare hands. The
beast collapsed. Dobrýnja let it live, however, on the condition that it stay
within its own borders, never to threaten humankind again.

Having extracted this promise, Dobrýnja returned to Kiev.
But it was unwise to put faith in the word of dragons. Gorynych soon took
revenge. Without warning, it descended on Kiev, lighting
on the palace at the city's heart. Then, roaring in triumph, it soared
above the white towers and gilded domes, its heads coiling among
the clouds. In its claws fluttered draperies of rose and gold: The dragon
had captured a Princess. It bore her screaming from view.

Then Dobrýnja left Kiev, armored and riding fast. He
rode like the wind to the mountains of Sorochinsk, crushing the serpents'
nests that littered his path. Into the lair of Gorynych the Wily
rode Dobrýnja, crying vengeance. And deep within a cavern he
found what he sought: The Princess of Kiev chained among hundreds of

her countrymen, whom the dragon had taken
on other forays. Dobrýnja freed the people and
turned to face the dragon. All
day the two battled under the staring sun. In the
end, the mortal killed Gorynych.
With a whip made of the silks of Samarkand,
he hewed off the heads and tails
and left them to wither. Then he set
the Princess in his saddle and brought her
back to her white-halled home.

Maeve what he planned. At last the Queen smiled. Her little King had his uses.

Together, then, Ailill and Maeve went to a river that meandered across the plain of Cruachan. In the middle of its current was an island. It was a sacred spot of ancient age, and near it in the water lurked its guardian, although none but Maeve and Ailill knew this.

Fróech was not far away. He had joined the warriors of Maeve and Ailill in a hunt, and the company was now resting in the shade of the trees, surrounded by panting hounds and sweating horses.

The Queen smiled upon him. "Let us make peace, young Prince," she said. "Agreements can be reached when hearts are willing, and my daughter may come to you yet." She sat down beside him on the grass, gave him her hand to kiss and began to chat of indifferent matters.

After a while, the Queen nodded toward the black water of the river and said, "We are told you are a great swimmer. Will you not show us?"

It was true that the Prince could swim, but he did so rarely, for it had been predicted that he would die by water. Maeve, with the help of her counselor birds, probably knew of the prophecy.

Fróech hesitated. "None of your men swim there. Is there harm in that water?"

"None that I know of," replied the Queen. "Do you fear it?"

For answer, Fróech stripped off his tunic and boots and dived into the water, stroking powerfully against the current.

"A strong swimmer, indeed," Maeve said. "Swim you to the island yonder?"

"I will."

"On the bank there grows a rowan tree," continued the Queen. "Bring me a branch of it, if you are brave enough." The rowan was a tree of life and had been since the time before men walked the earth. Its boughs and leaves and berries were said to have great power: They could give youth to the aged and protect mortals from evil. Hence the tree itself was sacred, hedged about with enchantment. Maeve wanted it for vigor in battle and also to ensure her own youth and beauty. But these were not her only reasons for asking the Prince to bring her a branch.

Fróech headed for the island. On the riverbank, Maeve's warriors rose slowly to their feet and clustered together, squinting into the sunshine. They murmured among themselves: None had ever dared to approach the island with its enchanted tree, for who could know what might happen when sacred places were defiled?

Fróech gained the island shore and walked from the water, tall and pale, his black hair gleaming. He snapped a red-berried sprig from the rowan tree. The warriors on the riverbank tensed, but nothing happened, and in another moment, the Prince had returned to the river.

He swam away from the island in easy strokes, the branch clasped in one hand. Then his head vanished and did not rise, and the black water boiled around the spot. Those on the riverbank saw a gleam of scales. They heard roaring. In moments, Fróech's head rose above the water again, and all could see the mighty fangs that were sunk into his shoulder and the

Death to a dragon from on high

Among dragonslayers, none possessed swiftness approaching that of Perseus, son of the god Zeus and the mortal Greek woman Danae. Perseus was beloved of the Olympian deities: They watched over him and bestowed on him such aids as winged shoes that permitted him to fly. Because of these shoes, he found a bride.

Once – that story begins – the shoes took him high over Ethiopia. As he flew, he spied far below him the shore of the Red Sea and, bound to a rock at the very edge of the waves, a maiden. Perseus descended and saw that she was beautiful. She told him a piteous tale. She was Andromeda, daughter of the rulers of the country, Cepheus and his wife Cassiopeia. On the advice of an oracle, Cepheus had set his daughter by the shore to serve as a sacrifice to a sea dragon that was ravaging his kingdom.

In an instant, Perseus sped to the King and said that he would slay the dragon in return for the hand of Andromeda. The King agreed to this. By the time Perseus returned to the place where he had left Andromeda, the beast had appeared. Screaming, it broke the surface of the water and cut through the foaming sea toward the maiden. With a stamp of his winged feet, Perseus rose into the air; he skimmed across the waves, hovered above the dragon's back and attacked it with his sword. The sea dragon lunged at him, but Perseus darted and stabbed like a wasp, always out of reach. The sword began to penetrate the thick hide here and there, and blood stained the water. At last the dragon heaved an awful sigh and sank beneath the waves.

And Perseus took Andromeda for his own that day.

120

It was said of Alexander the Great that he fought many dragons as he swept across the world. Advancing into India, his army was beset by boars, griffins and monstrous serpents. All were vanquished, like every human enemy who tried to thwart his drive for empire.

ribbons of blood, red as rowanberries, that streaked across his white flesh.

Fróech called out for a weapon. The Queen's warriors stooped to pick up their spears—and stopped at a gesture from the Queen. "Let him fight, if he is able," she said with a grim smile.

In an instant, Maeve was pushed to one side by a small figure. Findabair streaked by her, hair streaming gold. Where the maiden had come from, no one knew, but she bore Fróech's gold-hilted sword, and she dived into the river, making for the roiling, bloodied center where the Prince fought. Ailill cursed and cast a spear after her, aiming for the heart. He missed, and Findabair swam on.

It was impossible then to see how the fighting went, for the river foamed and roared. The golden head neared the place of battle; the black one rose beside it, and then Fróech's sword flashed in the air.

After some moments, Findabair sur-faced amid a drift of bloody bubbles near the riverbank. She turned her back on her parents and stood with the warriors. One of them covered her with his cloak.

At last the screaming and the roiling ceased. There was a moment so quiet that the people on the bank could hear a damsel fly as it danced above the surface of the water. Then the figure of Fróech appeared, standing upright in shallow water. His right hand was held high, brandishing an enormous head, scaled and white-eyed, the mouth gaping, the huge tongue lolling out. Black blood poured from the neck. And Fróech, too, was bleeding. Where his left arm had been was a gaping wound, glistening red around the white of shattered bone. The Prince lurched onto the bank and fell, and the dragon head rolled away from his loosened fingers. Fróech was dead, slain through the treachery of Maeve and Ailill.

So the young hero died, the best of Ireland, and the women of the Tuatha came to bear him away, keening as they went. Some chroniclers said that the fairy women restored him to life and health, and that Maeve and Ailill paid a blood fine for their deed and gave the brave Findabair to him. But these accounts also said that Maeve had her revenge at last, for she sent Fróech into a battle he could not win, and rather than surrender, he died in the waters of a ford. Other accounts state that he never breathed again and that the maid Findabair mourned for him all her life through. In either case, the Prince had slain the dragon that guarded the rowan tree. Thus another forbidden instrument of magic fell into the hands of men.

It was not only princes and knights such as Fróech and Saint George who slew dragons. There were stories about ordinary folk who vanquished the beasts. In Somerset, for instance, people loved to repeat the tale of Shervage Wood. They said a woodcutter working in the forest once paused to rest upon a huge fallen log. The log began to wriggle underneath him, and without a thought, the man picked up his ax and hacked it in two. It was a dragon, and the man had killed it. (The tale was probably apocryphal, an invention of villagers mocking their masters: Its usual ending was that the two halves of the dragon ran around the countryside for days, unable to join together.)

It was also said of various wanderers that they had killed dragons by thrusting balls of pitch and straw down the beasts' throats; ignited by the furnace-like heat of the dragons' guts, the balls exploded, destroying the animals.

But humble folk did not ordinarily engage in battle in those days: That was the business of the nobility, and most dragons were killed with the weapons of war — broadswords and lances — wielded by men whose lifelong training had made them experts. With few exceptions, this discipline was granted only to the gentle-born.

Training was provided by a system called fosterage, in which children as young as seven were sent to live in the fortresses of kings and overlords, serving there as pages while they learned the lessons that led to knighthood. At night the boys served the lords and men at table and slept with the dogs in the rushes that carpeted the great halls. The days were devoted to schooling. The fledgling warriors spent hours in shadowy mews, surrounded by rows of perched and hooded birds, learning from the austringers — the master falconers — the art of hawking. In the fields they practiced hunting, first with humble spar hawks, and later with great tercel goshawks, and — if their rank was high enough — with peregrine falcons and even mighty eagles. Falconry was a sport, it is true, but learning to handle the difficult birds taught the boys patience and guile.

The children practiced on archery fields, where they sent arrows at straw-filled targets. And they spent hour after aching, sweating hour on horseback on the tilting fields, riding at wooden dummies painted to look like armed knights and at brass rings suspended in the air. They learned to balance a heavy lance with the horse's motion; they learned accurate

A prophet's daring ploy

In centuries past, people loved to tell the tale of the Hebrew prophet Daniel and how he bested a dragon. Although he was of a different religion, Daniel was once a trusted confidant of Astyages, King of Babylon. To Daniel's dismay the people of Babylon, in their ignorance, worshipped a dragon at that time. To put an end to this evil idolatry, Daniel told Astyages that he would slay the sacred dragon without the aid of sword or staff. And so he did. Daniel boiled pitch, fat and hair together and shaped them into solid balls. These he forced down the dragon's throat. The balls exploded in the heat of the beast's belly, and the dragon burst on the spot.

aim. On foot, the boys hacked at one another with blunted broadswords so weighty that they had to be held in both hands. They learned to control the swing of the mace—a murderously spiked ball of iron appended to a chain.

The end of all this was that the soft, childish muscles hardened, the vision sharpened, the coordination of the body became catlike. The boys grew into warriors—dangerous, combative men held in control by the rigid code of honor that governed chivalry.

The boys were trained to fight the wars that continually raged across Europe in those centuries—not only the Crusades, but battles between ever-shifting kingdoms and empires or even between petty barons. When there was no war, the warriors' leaders kept the knights in check with hunting and tournaments and other martial diversions. Or, like Saint George, the young men rode abroad to seek their fortunes, knights errant in search of the adventures that would bring them glory.

Such a one was a Danish knight, Sigurd the Volsung. Sigurd was trained as were others of his class, but there was a difference, although he did not know it: He was trained not for war, but to give him the wit and strength to slay a particular dragon. The tale of his adventure begins many years before his birth.

In the dawn of time, a dwarf King dwelled in a northern land near the top of the world. Like other dwarfs, the King was skilled in the crafts of civilization and wise in the secret ways of nature, but he was ruled entirely by greed. By contemptible means he amassed a hoard of elf gold in his hall, for which his son, equally greedy, murdered him. That son was named Fafnir, and he had a brother, Regin. Regin lusted after the bloodied gold, too, but he was a coward, and when Fafnir threatened him, he fled.

Dwarfs are long-lived. Centuries passed, and the dwarf King's hall fell to ruin. Fafnir retired with his precious treasure to a desolate place called Gnita Heath, not far from the crumbling hall. Devoured by anxiety for his treasure, he kept clear of all mortals in order to stay by the gold. But it was gold that had been stolen from elves, which meant that it had curious properties.

Fafnir the patricide, hater of dwarfs and men alike, lost any resemblance to dwarfs or to men. He gradually changed into a monster, a huge creature covered with scales and filled with venom as evil as his heart. The creature that lived alone in the cave on Gnita Heath was no longer a dwarf but a dragon, although the beast retained the age-old knowledge of the dwarf race.

As for Regin, he wandered the earth, consumed with greed and hatred and fear. His body was small and dark and twisted, and his demeanor was mean and dour, but Regin had skills with which to earn his keep. He taught people the crafts that were the inheritance of dwarfs—those of the smith, the physician and the harper. And he waited patiently for the day when he would discover a dragonslayer to revenge himself on his brother.

That day came in the time when a King called Hialprek ruled the land of the

Danes; he kept Regin in comfort, for Regin served him as a master smith. Hialprek married a woman called Hiordis, the widow of the hero of a great clan who had died on the field of battle. She had a son by the hero, and the son was Sigurd, the last of the Volsung line.

Hiordis bore other sons to the King she married, but none of them burned with the flame that was in Sigurd. As a child, he had been golden as the sun, strong and brave beyond his years. When the dwarf Regin first saw the sturdy lad, he knew that his dragonslayer had been born. His behavior did not change—he remained as sullen as ever—but Regin made his plans and waited with the infinite patience of a dwarf.

In the court of Hialprek, the child Sigurd lived happily, playing with his half brothers, learning the arts of the warriors. He grew quickly, and when he became a youth—skilled in the use of weaponry, but still undisciplined—Regin left his smithy and requested an audience with the King.

He told Hialprek that he was growing old, and he asked for a pupil, that he might pass on the wisdom of the dwarfs before he died. Hialprek granted the boon, and Regin named his pupil—Sigurd.

Regin had the boy for years. There was no love between them, for the dwarf retained his silent, sour temperament. But Regin was a patient teacher. Sigurd learned the harper's skills, and he sang his lays with a voice as beautiful as an enchanter's. He became a great smith—a valuable skill in the early days of iron—although he never matched his master. He learned the arts of healing and the mysteries of plants and herbs. Regin watched and waited until Sigurd, like any youth, began to show signs of restlessness.

One day, the dwarf lingered near the archery field where Sigurd practiced with his half brothers. When they had finished, the dwarf called the youth to him. Sigurd strode across the field, flinging himself down on the grass beside Regin.

"You are stronger and surer than the King's sons," observed the dwarf. For reply, Sigurd only laughed and rolled onto his back. What Regin said was true, but Sigurd had a sunny nature; besides, he loved his half brothers. He did not care to hear them slighted.

"They will be kings, but you will have nothing," remarked the dwarf. "The son of a hero should be more than a knight at a small provincial court." Sigurd did not reply; he shrugged and then left, but the seed had been planted.

Some days later, Sigurd appeared at the door to the smithy, blinking in the firelit darkness, for the day outside was a bright one. The dwarf glanced up, and the fire of the forge made ugly shadows on his face. He said nothing, but he laid down the ringing hammer he wielded.

"What else should I do but stay here?" asked Sigurd, without preamble.

"Seek your own way in the world," replied the dwarf. "Find adventure, follow fame." He picked up the hammer again, but Sigurd asked, "Shall I go to serve a greater king?"

"A man who would be powerful finds his own way, not the path of another," answered the dwarf.

Few knew the profound power of the blood of dragons. But the hero Sigurd discovered the secret: The merest taste endowed a man with knowledge of ancient things of the earth.

"What, then?" asked Sigurd.

Regin sat down and wiped his hands. "Sit," he said. For some moments he stared into the fire. "I have been wronged," he began at last. Then he told how his brother had killed their father and stolen the gold that should have been shared. He told how Fafnir had become a dragon.

And Regin told Sigurd that the slaying of the dragon and the retrieval of the gold would be enough to make the young man a great lord in his own right. For himself, Regin said, he did not care about the gold: He wanted only the dragon's heart to eat, to regain the ancient dwarf wisdom that he had lost after so many years of teaching men. But that was a lie. Regin wanted the gold more than life itself; he wanted it as much as he wanted Fafnir's death.

But Sigurd was young and rash, and he did not see the greedy glitter in the dwarf's eyes, or notice the whine Regin's voice took on when he spoke of gold. "I will slay the dragon if you will make me a sword," Sigurd said.

Regin agreed to do that. He labored for weeks in the smoking forge, fashioning a mighty broadsword, and when it was ready, he summoned Sigurd. The youth tested the balance of the sword and ran his fingers lightly along its gleaming edge. Then he raised it high above his head and brought it down upon the smith's anvil. The blade shattered at the blow.

"This sword is not proof against dragons," Sigurd said and left the smithy.

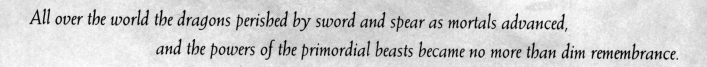

*All over the world the dragons perished by sword and spear as mortals advanced,
and the powers of the primordial beasts became no more than dim remembrance.*

Then Regin, cursing in his heart, made a second sword. This, too, the young man shattered. The dwarf said, "You have grown too strong for my weapons. Go to your mother and ask what she has for a son who has become a man."

Sigurd found his mother, Hiordis, in the weaving chamber of the palace, working with her women. When she saw her son's face, she set down her silver shuttle and rose from her loom at once: Hiordis, widow of a hero and wife of a King, knew what Sigurd wanted. She led the youth to her bedchamber and opened her painted bride chest. From among the stiff woolen robes and the folded linen Hiordis drew a bundle that was wrapped in silk.

"This is all that remains of the sword of the Volsung, your father's sword, broken in battle," she said. "It is for your own fame now. It is called Gram."

Sigurd drew back the silk and found only shards of steel. But they gave off their own light, for the Volsung sword had magic power. He left his mother and carried the broken blade to Regin. The dwarf nodded silently at what he saw. He took the pieces and from them forged the finest work ever made by dwarfs—a blade that was as strong as any on earth. He gave the blade a jeweled hilt.

Sigurd tried that sword upon the dwarf's anvil, and this time the anvil shattered at the bite of the blade. He laughed trium-

phantly, but no answering laugh came from Regin. "It is time to go," the dwarf said brusquely. He was thinking of the gold hoard, and his hands trembled with fear of the dragon.

So the two rode away from Hialprek's court, Sigurd on a great gray charger, the dwarf on his mule. They rode north through forests and across broad plains, and at last they came to the rolling wilderness of Gnita Heath. In a valley there, they found the hall of the dwarf King. Its roof was open to the sky, and grass grew among the paving stones of the great hall. Birds nested in the hearth.

"That is my father's hall," said Regin somberly. "In the hill behind is the cave where Fafnir lairs, guarding the elf gold." And indeed, a scarred and blackened track led down the hill to a pool near the hall. It was the trail the dragon made when he came to drink.

The two rested near the ruined hall, and there they made their plans. Regin told Sigurd that he must kill with the first blow. If he merely wounded the beast, it would shower him with venom. And the blow must be a belly blow, for only there were the dragon's scales vulnerable to the blade.

That night Regin and Sigurd dug a pit at the base of the dragon's trail. In the hour before the sun rose, Sigurd lay on his back in the pit, the sword Gram at his side. Regin covered the youth with his cloak and with a thin layer of earth. Then the dwarf fled and left Sigurd to his fate.

It was cold and damp in that earthen grave. Sigurd waited, motionless. Small stirrings—movements of things that lived in the earth—brushed his arms and legs, but Sigurd set his teeth and gripped the sword more firmly.

At last, shortly after dawn, he heard a rumbling sound in the earth around him. The dragon was moving at a ponderous pace, placing one foot slowly in front of the other. Fighting the urge to leap out and face the beast, Sigurd waited in his musty hiding place.

The earth trembled as the dragon's forefeet passed on either side of the pit. The time to strike had not yet come. Then Sigurd heard pebbles clattering and felt a great weight as the dragon's belly slid above him. He thrust the sword blade upward through the cloak and through the earth above, up until he felt the blade shudder as it struck and then slide into the belly of the beast.

A howl sounded, and the great weight lifted. Sigurd leaped to his feet, moving cloak and earth aside with the sword. At the edge of the pit writhed the dragon Fafnir, a gaping hole in its belly, black bile pouring from its mouth. Only the eyes were mortal, dark and deep like Regin's eyes—and dying now.

Sigurd the Volsung leaned on his sword and stared at his victim. The morning mist lifted from the trail; in the trees, birds began to chatter and sing. Regin appeared, hunched and shivering. He gave the dragon a vicious kick, then smiled, a bleak and wintery smile. "Roast me my brother's heart, as you promised, that I might save the ancient wisdoms. Afterward, we can share out the treasure."

This Sigurd did. He cut the heart from the carcass—for the dwarf greatly feared to touch the dragon—and spitted it on a branch while Regin watched closely. Then he built a fire and crouched beside it to roast the meat.

It took some time for the heart to cook. The dwarf sat on the ground and began to nod. At length, Sigurd prodded the flesh with his finger to see whether it was cooked and firm, and he got a burn for his trouble. He put the blistered finger into his mouth.

At once the bird song rose in a babbling chorus around him. It was cacophony, and Sigurd winced at the sound. But then wonderment came over him. The dragon's heart had powers indeed, for he found that he was able to understand the song the birds were singing:

"There sits Sigurd, son of the Volsung and victim of Regin. As he planned from the moment he saw the child, Regin will slay Sigurd to have all the gold. The dwarf will never let his poor dupe live."

Sigurd rounded on the dwarf. Regin's eyes snapped open, and in them, the young man found the truth. He saw Regin's soul and flinched at the evil. Regin knew that Sigurd saw, and froze in his place. Sigurd raised the sword Gram and smote off Regin's head.

So at the hands of a mortal died the dragon Fafnir, one of the last foul members of an ancient race—and with him died his treacherous brother. Sigurd the Volsung lived on, and his adventures became the stuff of song and legend. But he never fought a dragon again.

All over Europe, the dragons were vanishing, defeated by the new-won strength of humankind. In mountain passes, the leathery bodies moldered, on piles of gems and hoards of gold; on remote and rocky islands, the huge skeletons bleached in the sun; on the ocean floor, pale, branching coral grew from the bones.

The dragon was driven from the increasingly settled earth, but the memories of dragon fighting and slaying endured. Old tales continued to be told, old memories cherished. And new tales—witty but false—were devised to terrify and entertain the storytellers' audiences, who delighted in the beasts their ancestors had conquered.

But in the tellings, the dragons gradually were diminished. They became earthbound beasts, mere animals—though powerful ones—that men seemed always able to destroy. The people who listened to the tales forgot the true dimensions of the foe and the wonder of the triumph.

For dragons were not the beasts they became in the tales. Even the least of them represented the last of the first world; even the smallest was disorder made incarnate. Each of the dragons that haunted the earth descended from the titans that had lived before time, from the race of Tiamat and Apep and Typhon, and other elemental powers—star eaters, storm bringers, riders of the clouds.

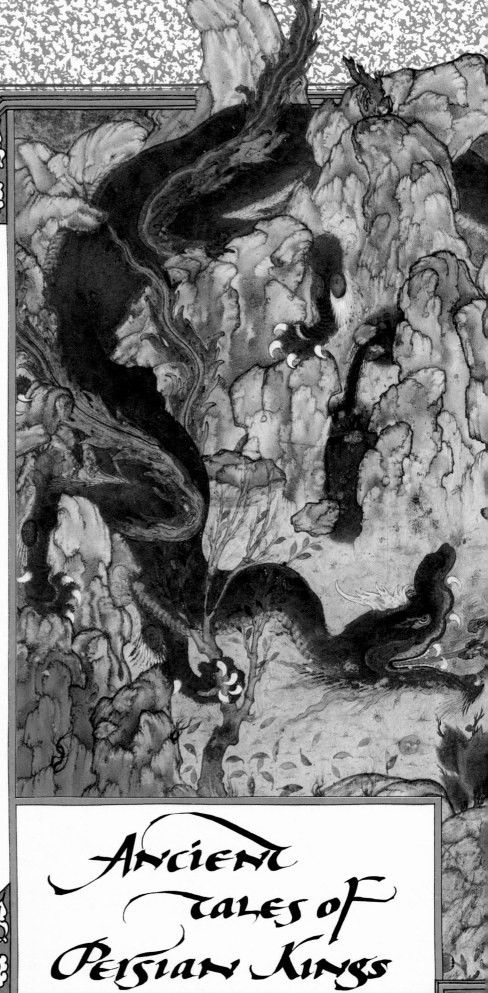

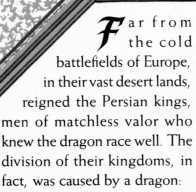

Far from the cold battlefields of Europe, in their vast desert lands, reigned the Persian kings, men of matchless valor who knew the dragon race well. The division of their kingdoms, in fact, was caused by a dragon:

At the beginning of history, there arose a mighty ruler called Faridun. He had three sons, whom he would not name until he knew their characters, which he discovered by appearing before the young men in the form of a flame-belching dragon. He challenged each son in turn. The first protested the folly of certain death—and fled. The second stood his ground, boasting that knight, lion and dragon were all one to him. The third invoked the name of Faridun and advised the beast to flee: He, the youth said, was Faridun's son.

So Faridun named his sons: The eldest he called Salm, for prudence, and gave his western territories. The middle son he named Tur, for bravery, and gave the eastern lands. The youngest one he called Iraj, for his discreet courage, and to him Faridun gave the world's jewel, Persia.

Ancient tales of Persian kings

Gushtasp the Valiant

Centuries passed, and Iraj's line continued to rule over Persia and to face dragons. But these dragons, unlike Faridun, were not visions or spiritual tests alone. They had to be slain.

Iraj's descendant Gushtasp, son of Lohrasp, killed a dragon to help another man pass a test. Gushtasp had married a Western Emperor's daughter against the Emperor's wishes and had been banished. Yet his fame as a huntsman spread far beyond the wilderness to which he and his bride had retired. And when the embittered Emperor set impossible tasks for his remaining daughters' suitors, Gushtasp accomplished them. He slew an elephant-sized wolf for one suitor and a six-legged dragon for another, first weakening it with a barrage of arrows, then affixing a many-bladed dagger to his spear and plunging the weapon down the dragon's throat.

Word soon spread that it was Gushtasp who had performed these heroic deeds. His father-in-law embraced him and made him general of the imperial army. And, finally, Gushtasp's father proudly called him home and stepped down, that Gushtasp might rule in his place.

Isfandiyar the Crafty

Gushtasp's son Isfandiyar overcame a dragon while journeying east to rescue his sisters from an invading warlord. The crafty Prince built a wooden carriage studded with sharp hooks and sword blades.

Then, concealed within, Isfandiyar fearlessly drove the boxlike contraption, horses and all, straight into the maw of the dragon.

The bristling carriage stuck there, choking and lacerating the throat of the beast, which retreated to free itself. Isfandiyar then sprang from the cart, drew his sword and split open the dragon's head.

Like the powerful Gushtasp, Isfandiyar's son Shah Ardashir met his dragon atop a mountain, and like Isfandiyar, he entered its jaws. But unlike his father, Ardashir never emerged.

Ardashir had been riding in the Zagros mountains when the beast surprised him from behind. Before he could flee, horse and rider were snapped up in a single bite, and Ardashir—who did not seek to challenge a dragon—became the only man of his line to die by one.

Ardashir the Unfortunate

Bahram Gur the Venturous

One spring, generations after Ardashir's death, Shah Bahram Gur collected his best marksmen, his trained panthers and his hawks for a hunt.

Within days, hill and plain were swept clean of onager, gazelle and sheep. The hunters were content – all but the Shah, who set off, alone, and

found a dragon. He shot one arrow at its chest, a second at its head. Then he gutted the beast and found, to his horror, a man's body in the belly.

Of all Persia's heroes, the greatest was Rustam, a feudal lord who was born in the reign of Manuchihr, Faridun's grandson.

Rustam had a dappled horse named Rakhsh, famous for loyalty. Rakhsh was an intrepid beast that always stood guard when the warrior camped for the night.

It happened once that a ferocious dragon crept into Rustam's camp while the warrior slept. The horse stamped its hoofs and whinnied, bringing the warrior from his tent – but by that time the dragon had retreated into invisibility, and the man rebuked the horse. Twice more the dragon approached, and twice more Rakhsh neighed and Rustam awoke – to see nothing. Each time Rustam grew angrier.

The next time the dragon slithered near, Rakhsh waited until the beast was within reach of its master's sword before sounding a warning whinny. Rustam – his sleep understandably light – leaped up and saw the dragon almost upon him.

The beast sprang and clasped the man within its powerful coils. But the strong teeth of the faithful horse fastened onto the dragon's side, and the monster relaxed its grip enough so that Rustam was able to free himself. With his scimitar, he slashed the dragon to death.

And then the Persian warrior Rustam sang a paean of thanks to Allah and praise to his valorous steed.

Acknowledgments

The editors are particularly indebted to John Dorst, consultant, for his help in the preparation of this volume. The editors also thank the following persons and institutions: François Avril, Chief Curator, Département des Manuscrits, Bibliothèque Nationale, Paris; Elena Bradunas, American Folklife Center, Library of Congress, Washington, D.C.; Nancy Cheng, East Asian Bibliographer, Van Pelt Library, University of Pennsylvania, Philadelphia; Jean-Paul Desroches, Curator, Musée Guimet, Paris; Volker Dünnhaupt, Bibliothek, Rheinisches Landesmuseum, Bonn; Laveta Emory, the Freer Gallery of Art, Washington, D.C.; Clark Evans, Rare Book and Special Collections Division, Library of Congress, Washington, D.C.; Marielise Göpel, Archiv für Kunst und Geschichte, West Berlin; Francis Gueth, Curator, Bibliothèque Municipale, Colmar, France; Dieter Hennig, Director, Gebrüder-Grimm Museum, Kassel, Germany; Christine Hoffmann, Bayerische Staatsgemäldesammlungen, Munich; Arthur A. Houghton Jr., Wye Plantation, Queenstown, Maryland; Lydia Hsieh, Assistant Librarian, the Freer Gallery of Art, Washington, D.C.; Huang Yung-Sung, Art Director, *Echo* magazine, Taipei; Ann Huey, Potomac, Maryland; Heidi Klein, Bildarchiv Preussischer Kulturbesitz, West Berlin; Roland Klemig, Bildarchiv Preussischer Kulturbesitz, West Berlin; Library Staff, The Central Art Academy of Beijing; Li Lin-Tsan, Deputy Director, National Palace Museum, Taipei; Glenise A. Matheson, Keeper of Manuscripts, The John Rylands University Library, Manchester, England; Ellen Nollman, Head Librarian, the Freer Gallery of Art, Washington, D.C.; Princeton Index of Christian Art, Vatican City; Lores Riva, Milan; Justin Schiller, New York City; Johannes A. Seifert, Bibliothek, Rheinisches Landesmuseum, Bonn; Robert Shields, Rare Book and Special Collections Division, Library of Congress, Washington, D.C.; Marie Lukens Swietochowski, Associate Curator, Islamic Division, Metropolitan Museum of Art, New York City; Peter Tange and Burg Wissem, Troisdorf, Germany.

Picture Credits

Credits from left to right are separated by semicolons, from top to bottom by dashes. When known, the artist's name precedes the picture source.

Cover: Karl Dielitz, courtesy Archiv für Kunst und Geschichte, West Berlin. 1-5: Artwork by Wayne Anderson. 6, 7: Artwork by John Jude Palencar. 10: Bodleian Library, Oxford, Ms. Douce. 167.f.10R. 12, 13: Artwork by Wayne Anderson. 15: Johann Heinrich Fuseli, courtesy the Royal Academy of Arts, London; artwork by Kinuko Y. Craft. 16, 17: Artwork by Kinuko Y. Craft. 18, 19: Artwork by Alicia Austin. 21: National Gallery of Prague Collection, courtesy Werner Forman Archive, London. 22, 23: From *Arthur Rackham's Book of Pictures*, William Heinemann, 1913, by permission of Barbara Edwards, courtesy Victoria and Albert Museum, London. 25: Salvator Rosa, courtesy The Montreal Museum of Fine Arts, donation of Miss Olive Hosmer. 26: Edmund Dulac, courtesy Prints Division, Astor, Lenox and Tilden Foundations, The New York Public Library, photographed by Philip Pocock. 28, 29: Andreas Cellarius, courtesy Rare Book and Special Collections Division, Library of Congress. 30-39: Artwork by Wayne Anderson. 40, 41: Artwork by Kinuko Y. Craft. 43: Artwork by Jill Karla Schwarz. 44-53: Artwork by Sharleen Collicott. 54, 55: Artwork by Jill Karla Schwarz. 56, 57: Courtesy the Freer Gallery of Art, Smithsonian Institution, Washington, D.C. 58, 59: Ichiyūsai Kuniyoshi gwa, courtesy Victoria and Albert Museum, London. 60: Courtesy the Freer Gallery of Art, Smithsonian Institution, Washington, D.C. 62-69: Artwork by Kinuko Y. Craft. 70, 71: Martin Riester, courtesy Bibliothèque Municipale de Colmar, photographed by Christian Kempf, Colmar. 74, 75: Artwork by John Jude Palencar. 77-87: Artwork by Judy King-Rieniets. 90, 91: Walter Crane, courtesy Sotheby Parke Bernet & Co., London. 92, 93: Artwork by Rallé. 95: Raphael, courtesy Cliché des Musées Nationaux, Paris. 96: Artwork by Teresa Fasolino. 98-105: Artwork by James C. Christensen. 106, 107: Pinacoteca Toso-Martinengo, Brescia, courtesy Fabbri, Milan. 110: Dante Gabriel Rossetti, courtesy The Tate Gallery, London. 112: Arthur Rackham, from *The Romance of King Arthur and His Knights of the Round Table*, abridged from Malory's *Morte d'Arthur* by A. W. Pollard, Macmillan and Co., 1917, by permission of Barbara Edwards, courtesy Victoria and Albert Museum, London. 115-118: Artwork by Alicia Austin. 120, 121: Piero di Cosimo, Galleria degli Uffizi, courtesy Scala, Florence. 122: Ville de

Bibliography

Alexander, Alex E., *Russian Folklore: An Anthology in English Translation*. Belmont, Massachusetts: Nordland Publishing, 1975.

Allen, Judy, and Jeanne Griffiths, *The Book of the Dragon*. London: Orbis Publishing, 1979.

Allen, Richard Hinckley, *Star-Names and Their Meanings*. New York: G. E. Stechert, 1936 (reprint of 1899 edition).

Baring-Gould, Sabine, *Curious Myths of the Middle Ages*. Ed. by Edward Hardy. London: Jupiter Books, 1977.

Beowulf. Transl. by David Wright. Baltimore: Penguin Books, 1973 (reprint).

Birch, Cyril, *Chinese Myths and Fantasies*. New York: Henry Z. Walck, 1961.

Briggs, Katharine M., *A Dictionary of British Folk-Tales in the English Language*. London: Routledge & Kegan Paul, 1971.

Bulfinch, Thomas:
Bulfinch's Mythology. New York: The Modern Library, no date.
Myths of Greece and Rome. Compiled by Bryan Holme. New York: Penguin Books, 1981.

Campbell, J. F., *The Celtic Dragon Myth*. Transl. by George Henderson. North Hollywood, California: Newcastle Publishing, 1981.

Cavendish, Richard, ed.:
Man, Myth & Magic. 11 vols. New York: Marshall Cavendish, 1983.
Mythology: An Illustrated Encyclopedia. London: Orbis Publishing, 1980.

Clark, Anne, *Beasts and Bawdy*. New York: Taplinger Publishing, 1975.

Coolidge, Olivia E., *Legends of the North*. Boston: Houghton Mifflin, 1951.

Davis, F. Hadland, *Myths & Legends of Japan*. London: George G. Harrap, 1912.

Dickinson, Peter, *The Flight of Dragons*. London: Pierrot Publishing, 1979.

Doble, Gilbert H., *The Saints of Cornwall*, Pt. 4. Oxford: The Holywell Press, 1965 (reprint).

Doria, Charles, and Harris Lenowitz, eds. and transls., *Origins: Creation Texts from the Ancient Mediterranean*. New York: Anchor Books, 1976.

Downing, Charles, *Russian Tales and Legends*. Oxford University Press, 1978 (reprint).

Eberhard, Wolfram, *Studies in Chinese Folklore and Related Essays*. Bloomington: Indiana University Research Center for the Language Sciences, 1970.

Eberhard, Wolfram, ed., *Folktales of China* (Folktales of the World series). The University of Chicago Press, 1965.

Edwards, E. D., ed. and compiler, *The Dragon Book*. London: William Hodge, no date.

Ferdowsi, *The Epic of the Kings: Shah-Nama, the National Epic of Persia* (Persian Heritage series). Transl. by Reuben Levy. London: Routledge & Kegan Paul, 1967.

Fontenrose, Joseph, *Python: A Study of Delphic Myth and Its Origins*. Berkeley: University of California Press, 1959.

Fox-Davies, A. C., *A Complete Guide to Heraldry*. London: Thomas Nelson and Sons, 1969 (reprint of 1909 edition).

Gantz, Jeffrey, transl., *The Mabinogion*. New York: Penguin Books, 1981 (reprint).

Garmonsway, G. N., transl., *The Anglo-Saxon Chronicle*. London: J. M. Dent & Sons, 1965 (reprint).

Geoffrey of Monmouth, *The History of the Kings of Britain*. Transl. by Lewis Thorpe. New York: Penguin Books, 1982 (reprint).

George, Wilma, *Animals and Maps*. Berkeley: University of California Press, 1969.

Gordon-Smith, Richard, *Ancient Tales and Folklore of Japan*. London: A. & C. Black, 1908.

Gould, Charles:
The Dragon. Ed. by Malcolm Smith. London: Wildwood House, 1977.
Mythical Monsters. Detroit: Singing Tree Press, 1969 (reprint of

1886 edition).

Graves, Robert, *The Greek Myths*, Vols. 1 and 2. New York: Penguin Books, 1979 and 1980 (reprints).

Green, Roger Lancelyn, *Heroes of Greece and Troy*. New York: Henry Z. Walck, 1961.

Green, Roger Lancelyn, ed., *A Cavalcade of Dragons*. New York: Henry Z. Walck, 1970.

Grimm, Jacob and Wilhelm:
The Complete Grimm's Fairy Tales. Transl. by Margaret Hunt. New York: Pantheon Books, 1944.
Sixty Fairy Tales of the Brothers Grimm. Transl. by Alice Lucas. New York: Weathervane Books, 1979.

Hawthorne, Nathaniel, *A Wonder-Book and Tanglewood Tales*. Boston: Houghton Mifflin, 1951 (reprint).

Heller, Julek, *Knights*. New York: Schocken Books, 1982.

Henderson, William, *Notes on the Folk-Lore of the Northern Counties of England and the Borders*. London: W. Satchell, Peyton, 1879.

Hogarth, Peter, with Val Clery, *Dragons*. New York: The Viking Press, 1979.

Hoke, Helen, ed., *Dragons, Dragons, Dragons*. New York: Franklin Watts, 1972.

Hole, Christina, *Saints in Folklore*. New York: M. Barrows, 1965.

Holman, Felice, and Nanine Valen, *The Drac: French Tales of Dragons and Demons*. New York: Charles Scribner's Sons, 1975.

Huxley, Francis, *The Dragon: Nature of Spirit, Spirit of Nature*. London: Thames and Hudson, 1979.

Ingersoll, Ernest, *Dragons and Dragon Lore*. New York: Payson & Clarke, 1928.

Johnsgard, Paul and Karin, *Dragons and Unicorns: A Natural History*. New York: St. Martin's Press, 1982.

Joly, Henri L., *Legend in Japanese Art*. Rutland, Vermont: Charles E. Tuttle, 1967.

Lang, Andrew, ed., *The Violet Fairy Book*. New York: Dover Publications, 1966 (reprint of 1901 edition).

Leach, Maria, ed., *Funk & Wagnalls Standard Dictionary of Folklore, Mythology and Legend*. 2 vols. New York: Funk & Wagnalls, 1950.

Leeming, David, *Mythology*. New York: Newsweek Books, 1975.

Lim Sian-tek, *Folk Tales from China*. New York: The John Day Company, 1944.

The Literature of Persia, Pt. 1. Freeport, New York: Books for Libraries Press, 1971 (reprint of 1900 edition).

Malory, Sir Thomas, *Le Morte Darthur*. Ed. by R. M. Lumiansky. New York: Charles Scribner's Sons, 1982.

Mary Catherine, Sister, *Once in Cornwall*. New York: Longmans, Green, 1944.

Medieval Epics: Beowulf. Transl. by William Alfred. New York: The Modern Library, 1963.

New Larousse Encyclopedia of Mythology. Transl. by Richard Aldington and Delano Ames. London: The Hamlyn Publishing Group, 1974.

Newman, Paul, *The Hill of the Dragon: An Enquiry into the Nature of Dragon Legends*. Totowa, New Jersey: Rowman and Littlefield, 1980.

Rowling, Marjorie, *Life in Medieval Times*. New York: Perigee Books, 1968.

Sanders, Tao Tao Liu, *Dragons, Gods & Spirits from Chinese Mythology*. New York: Schocken Books, 1983.

Schwab, Gustav, *Gods & Heroes: Myths and Epics of Ancient Greece*. Transl. by Olga Marx and Ernst Morwitz. New York: Pantheon Books, 1974.

Scott, Allan, and Michael Scott Rohan, *Fantastic People*. London: Pierrot Publishing, 1980.

Seki, Keigo, ed., *Folktales of Japan* (Folktales of the World series). Transl. by Robert J. Adams. The University of Chicago Press, 1963.

Smith, G. Elliot, *The Evolution of the Dragon*. London: Longmans, Green, 1919.

Spicer, Dorothy Gladys, *13 Dragons*. New York: Coward, McCann & Geoghegan, 1974.

Steep, Thomas, *Chinese Fantastics*. New York: The Century Company, 1925.

Sturluson, Snorri, *The Prose Edda*. Transl. by Arthur Gilchrist Brodeur. New York: The American-Scandinavian Foundation, 1967.

Titley, Norah M., *Dragons in Persian, Mughal and Turkish Art*. London: The British Library, 1981.

Topsell, Edward, *Topsell's Histories of Beasts*. Ed. by Malcolm South. Chicago: Nelson-Hall, 1981.

Vinycomb, John, *Fictitious & Symbolic Creatures in Art with Special Reference to Their Use in British Heraldry*. Detroit: Gale Research, 1969 (reprint of 1906 edition).

Visser, M. W. de, *The Dragon in China and Japan*. Weisbaden: Martin Sändig, 1969.

Welch, Stuart Cary:
A King's Book of Kings: The Shah-Nameh of Shah Tahmasp. London: Thames and Hudson, 1972.
Royal Persian Manuscripts. London: Thames and Hudson, 1976.

Werner, E. T. C.:
A Dictionary of Chinese Mythology. New York: The Julian Press, 1961 (reprint of 1932 edition).
Myths & Legends of China. New York: Farrar & Rinehart, 1933.

Westwood, Jennifer, transl., *Medieval Tales*. New York: Coward-McCann, 1968.

White, T. H., *The Goshawk*. New York: Penguin Books, 1979.

White, T. H., ed., *The Bestiary: A Book of Beasts, Being a Translation from a Latin Bestiary of the Twelfth Century*. New York: Capricorn Books (G. P. Putnam's Sons), 1960.

Williams, C. A. S., *Outlines of Chinese Symbolism and Art Motives*. 3rd ed. New York: Dover Publications, 1976.

Time-Life Books Inc.
is a wholly owned subsidiary of

TIME INCORPORATED

FOUNDER: Henry R. Luce 1898-1967

Editor-in-Chief: Henry Anatole Grunwald
President: J. Richard Munro
Chairman of the Board: Ralph P. Davidson
Corporate Editor: Jason McManus
Group Vice President, Books: Joan D. Manley

TIME-LIFE BOOKS INC.

EDITOR: George Constable
Executive Editor: George Daniels
Director of Design: Louis Klein
Editorial Board: Dale M. Brown,
Robert G. Mason, Ellen Phillips,
Peter Pocock, Gerry Schremp,
Gerald Simons, Rosalind Stubenberg,
Kit van Tulleken, Henry Woodhead
Director of Administration: David L. Harrison
Director of Research: Phyllis K. Wise
Director of Photography: John Conrad Weiser

PRESIDENT: Reginald K. Brack Jr.
Senior Vice President: William Henry
Vice Presidents: George Artandi,
Stephen L. Bair, Robert A. Ellis,
Juanita T. James, Christopher T. Linen,
James L. Mercer, Joanne A. Pello,
Paul R. Stewart

THE ENCHANTED WORLD

SERIES DIRECTOR: Ellen Phillips
Deputy Editor: Robin Richman
Designer: Dale Pollekoff
Chief Researcher: Jane Edwin

Editorial Staff for *Dragons*
Staff Writers: Tim Appenzeller,
Donald Davison Cantlay,
David S. Thomson
Researchers: Norma E. Kennedy (principal),
Scarlet Cheng, Gregory A. McGruder
Assistant Designer: Lorraine D. Rivard
Copy Coordinators: Anthony K. Pordes,
Barbara Fairchild Quarmby
Picture Coordinator: Nancy C. Scott
Editorial Assistant: Constance B. Strawbridge

Special Contributors: Ann Kuhns Corson,
John Drummond

Editorial Operations
Design: Ellen Robling (assistant director)
Copy Room: Diane Ullius
Production: Anne B. Landry (director),
Celia Beattie
Quality Control: James J. Cox (director),
Sally Collins
Library: Louise D. Forstall

Correspondents: David Aikman (Beijing);
Elisabeth Kraemer-Singh (Bonn); Margot
Hapgood, Dorothy Bacon (London);
Miriam Hsia (New York); Maria Vincenza
Aloisi, Josephine du Brusle (Paris); Ann
Natanson (Rome).
Valuable assistance was also provided by:
Jaime FlorCruz, Kosima Weber Liu (Beijing);
Angelika Lemmer (Bonn); Marie Gerald
(Boston); Bing Wong (Hong Kong); Lesley
Coleman (London); Carolyn Chubet
(New York); Ann Wise (Rome); Traudl
Lessing (Vienna).

Chief Series Consultant

Tristram Potter Coffin, Professor of
English at the University of Pennsylvania, is a leading authority on folklore. He is the author or editor of
numerous books and more than 100 articles. His best-known works are *The
British Traditional Ballad in North America,
The Old Ball Game, The Book of Christmas
Folklore* and *The Female Hero.*

This volume is one of a series that
is based on myths, legends and folk tales.

Other Publications:

THE KODAK LIBRARY OF CREATIVE PHOTOGRAPHY
GREAT MEALS IN MINUTES
THE CIVIL WAR
PLANET EARTH
COLLECTOR'S LIBRARY OF THE CIVIL WAR
LIBRARY OF HEALTH
CLASSICS OF THE OLD WEST
THE EPIC OF FLIGHT
THE GOOD COOK
THE SEAFARERS
WORLD WAR II
HOME REPAIR AND IMPROVEMENT
THE OLD WEST
LIFE LIBRARY OF PHOTOGRAPHY (revised)
LIFE SCIENCE LIBRARY (revised)

For information on and a full description
of any of the Time-Life Books series listed
above, please write:
Reader Information
Time-Life Books
541 North Fairbanks Court
Chicago, Illinois 60611

Library of Congress Cataloguing in
Publication Data
Main entry under title:
Dragons
  (The Enchanted world)
  Bibliography: p.
  1. Dragons. 2. Tales. I. Time-Life Books.
II. Series.
GR830.D7D73 1984   398.2'454   84-2646
ISBN 0-8094-5208-1
ISBN 0-8094-5209-X (lib. bdg.)

Time-Life Books Inc. offers a wide range of
fine recordings, including a *Big Bands* series.
For subscription information, call 1-800-621-
7026 or write TIME-LIFE MUSIC, Time &
Life Building, Chicago, Illinois 60611.